LET'S GO TO THE PICTURES...

A HUNDRED YEARS
OF
CINEMAS IN KETTERING

SOUVENIR

SAVOY CINEMA

OPENED

SATURDAY

MAY 21st, 1938

LET'S GO TO THE PICTURES...

A HUNDRED YEARS
OF
CINEMAS IN KETTERING

MAURICE THORNTON

HOODED LION BOOKS
KETTERING
NORTHAMPTONSHIRE
2000

First published 2000

ISBN 0 9537037 2 X

Published by
Hooded Lion Books
147 Russell Street
KETTERING
Northamptonshire NN16 0EW
Hooded Lion Books is an Imprint of
Monkshood Publishing

Printed and Bound in Great Britain by
Woolnough Bookbinding
IRTHLINGBOROUGH
Northamptonshire NN9 5SE

Set in Raleigh and Times New Roman

This Book is dedicated to

David Norman

ACKNOWLEDGEMENTS

My thanks go to the following who without their help, contribution and encouragement, this book could not have been written:

R. W. Anderson, General Manager, Wicksteed Park, Kettering; David Allen; Douglas Ashby; the late Colin Ball; Colin Bamford; David Bradshaw, *My Technicolor Boulevard*; Alah Buksh; Mrs P. Christie, Scunthorpe; P. Cowan; Mrs P. Cowan; J. Copley; Carmel Crawley, Librarian, Northamptonshire Newspapers Limited, for her valued assistance; Janene Cox, Principal Librarian, Kettering Library; Sue Davies, Heritage Manager, Kettering Museum; Mavis Dodson; George Dunkley; Irene Faller; Jim Filby; Mr and Mrs Reg Goodman; Tom Haycock; S. M. Irons; Brian McFarlane; Margaret McManus; C. T. Marlow; Geoff Marlow; Sheila Milligan; B. G. Old; Malcolm Robinson, Kettering Reference Library, for his most professional assistance; Lewis J. Stanley; Charles W. Thurston, Thurston Amusements (Great Yarmouth) Limited; Beryl Tiney; Eddie Toseland; W. A. S. Wakefield, Kettering Industrial Cooperative Society Limited; Miss R. Watson, Northamptonshire County Archivist; R.D. Wharton; Stan White, Historian; S. J. Winfield; Marion Williams.

The British Film Institute; The *Evening Telegraph*, Northamptonshire Newspapers Limited; Brian Hornsey, *Ninety Years of Cinema in Kettering*; KCBC Radio, Kettering; Rank Leisure Limited, especially Adrian Duffey, Bradley Salmon, David Pryke and Richard Vowles; Photo Coverage.

The person who kindly sent to me, anonymously, The Savoy opening souvenir programme.

Anyone else who I may have inadvertently omitted.

Every effort has been made to trace all the copyright owners of the material used, but if any have been inadvertently overlooked, the author and publisher will be pleased to make the necessary arrangement at the first opportunity.

PREFACE

From the 1930s to the 1960s, Kettering cinemas hold a special place in my life. Like so many of my generation they were a part of my childhood, growing up and youth. Their influence continued into adult life, and up to the present day. Going to the pictures is still an occasion for me, even though I continue to work as a projectionist. But it always was an occasion. To have worked at one time in a Kettering cinema, especially as it was boyhood favourite, was a pleasure no other period of my working life has ever matched.

I was sent an article from the local paper some years ago, which told of the closing of The *Granada*, the cinema in which I had worked. I realised that little had been recorded about the six cinemas Kettering once had, and became aware that if something was not done soon, the story of the Kettering cinemas and their contribution to the life of the town would be lost forever.

Whilst researching I quickly realised that each cinema had a fascinating story. The buildings, the people that built them and ran them, the personalities that emerged, and of course the character and style of the cinemas themselves, all contributed to the period in which they existed.

Research was rewarding, if difficult. So many cinema veterans had gone, but those who have responded to numerous appeals and my trawling of the local papers have brought memories flooding back of the thirty-five years or so I lived in the town.

There are few reminders of cinema heritage in Kettering at the turn of the century. Some of the buildings have since gone, one is threatened, and *all* have other uses. Future generations will have little knowledge of where The *Savoy*,

Regal, Gaumont, Empire or old *Odeon* were, or even of their existence; nor of the Working Men's Club and its cinema. Good reason then to write this book and I hope it gives as much pleasure and enjoyment to readers as it has to me in researching and writing it.

This book has been written using the fundamental research of the late Colin Ball and the published work *Ninety Years of Cinema* in Kettering by Brian Hornsey, and has been developed with additional research by the author using newspaper files, writings, memories of contributors responding to appeals, and by my own diligence. Views expressed are those of the author and not necessarily by contributors and previous researchers.

This book is compiled from material researched to December 1997. Differences to research previously published by others does not, nor is intended, to invalidate such research and recording.

Every effort has been made to verify and authenticate the information contained in the book. It must be appreciated though, that in a work of this depth some omissions and errors may occur for which apologies are expressed.

Also, the photographs and illustrations have sometimes been hard to come by. Consequently, some of the photographs in the book are not of the quality I should have liked – but it is the best we can do. I hope that my readers understand this, and look upon the illustrations with a kindly eye.

Students of cinema and media subjects who are undertaking research on, or reading about, the cinemas of Kettering and district, or indeed any cinema, are invited to seek further information from the Author.

Maurice Thornton,
5 Birdcombe Close,
Nailsea,
Bristol BS48 1HH.

November 1999

CONTENTS

LIST OF SUBSCRIBERS

David and Anne Allen, Kettering
Mr Douglas Ashby, Burton Latimer
Colin Bamford, Hope Valley, Australia
Dennis Cowen, Kettering
The Curzon Community Cinema, Clevedon, Bristol
Stephen Colin Dimond, Clevedon
Mavis Dodson (nee Varnfield), Kettering
Kenneth J. Draper, Milton Keynes
Hugh Gibbs, Knutsford
Chris Godbold and Trevor Haynes, Great Oakley
Astrid and David Hendra, Clevedon
Anthony Irving, West Quantoxhead
Ann and Alan Joyce, Rothwell
Joe and thomas Knowles, Eastville, Bristol
C. T. Marlow, Clevedon
Timothy McCullen, Sevenoaks
C. D. Morris, Grangeover Sands
John Muggleton, Boston
John Norman, Rothwell
Jonathan Norman, Grimston, Norfolk
Andrew Reed, Clevedon
Ken Roe, London
George Brent Skelly, London
David Smith, London
Trevor and Diana Smith, Rothwell
P. W. Spenceley, Nailsea
Barry Stevenson, London
Neville C. Taylor, London
Carol Thornton, Nailsea
Joyce Thornton, Nailsea
Lynn Thornton, Clevedon
Simon James Thornton, Nailsea
Jonathan Walker, Wellingborough
Stan White, Rothwell

CHRONOLOGY

1897	
Feast Week, July	Taylor's Bioscope at the Fairground on the Recreation Ground, Northampton Road. First paying public shows of the cinematograph in Kettering.
Thursday 2 December	'Animated pictures' shown at the Oddfellows' Hall in Desborough. Probably the first 'cinema show' to a paying audience within a building in the area.
1901	
Tuesday/Wednesday 12/13 March	Victoria Hall: Warren East 'Living Pictures' cinematograph show
Feast Week, July	Charles Thurston's *Original Royal Show* Bioscope first appearance in Kettering
1902	Work begins on Kettering's first purpose built theatre in Russell Street
1903	
Tuesday 3 February	Corn Exchange: Jasper Redfern presents the Electric Dissolving Stereoscope 'Animated Pictures' and the American Vaudeville Show
Monday 3 August	The *Avenue* theatre in Russell Street opens
1907	
Feast Week, July	William Taylor presents his mammoth Bioscope and Fair Organ featuring the new 'Chronomegaphone' sound pictures at the Fair ground, Northampton Road
1908	
Feast Week, July	Charles Thurston presents his new *Royal Show* Bioscope and variety
November	The *Avenue* theatre closes and re-opens as a roller-skating rink
1909	
October	Leo Vint takes over the Corn Exchange and converts to a cinema. Opens as *Vint's Electric Palace*

1910

October	The *Avenue* closes as a roller-skating rink
Friday 14 October	The *Avenue* re-opens as a theatre under the name of The *Coliseum*
1912	*Vint's Electric Palace* taken over by Covington, and renamed The *Palace*
	The Oddfellows' Hall, Desborough leased by Mr and Mrs Jackson, and opens as The *Electric Picture Palace*
1913	
Saturday 10 May	Kettering's first purpose-built cinema Kettering *Electric Pavilion* opens
1914	
August	New built *Electric Palace* at Burton Latimer starts operating
Monday 2 November	and opens officially
1917	
November	Fred Hawkins takes over The *Palace* renaming it The *Hippodrome*
1919	
August	*Kettering Electric Pavilion* changes hands and is renamed The *Electric Pavilion*
1920	
Monday 3 May	Kettering's second purpose built cinema The Empire opens in Eskdail Street Victoria Hall closes for reconstruction as a cinema
Monday 23 August	The *Victoria Picture House* opens
August	The *Picture House*, Rothwell opens
1921	
January	The *Hippodrome* ceases publicity, and possibly closes. Business dissolved in February
1924	Alfred Watts purchases The *Electric Palace*, Burton Latimer
1927	The *Electric Pavilion* taken over by Gaumont-British Picture Corporation and renamed The *Gaumont Pavilion*
1929	
Friday 31 May	The *Coliseum* up for auction, fails to meet the reserved price
Monday 9 December	The *Gaumont Pavilion* opens after conversation to 'talkies' with *Perfect Alibi*

Chronology

1931	
Monday 4 May	The *Empire* converts to sound and opens with *Let Us Be Gay*
1932	The *Coliseum* closes. Jack Sherwood takes control
Wednesday 3 August	The *Coliseum* re-opens with new name The *New Coliseum*
1933	
Christmas	The cinema at the Working Men's Club in Wellington Street begins advertising 'talkies'
1936	
Friday 24 April	The *Victoria Picture House* closes, and work begins on conversion to The *Odeon*
Saturday 19 September	The *Odeon* opens with *Strike Me Pink*
Saturday 26 December	The *Regal* super cinema opens with spectacular show, and the film *Everything Is Rhythm*
1937	
Tuesday 6 April	The *New Coliseum* gutted by fire
|Saturday 1 May	Jack Sherwood takes over The *Empire*
November	Claude Copley takes over The *Electric Palace* at Desborough, modernizes and re-opens the cinema as The *Ritz*
1938	
Saturday 21 May	The *Savoy* theatre/cinema opens on the old *New Coliseum* site with Jack Sherwood as owner
1939	
Sunday 3 September	Second World War declared. All cinemas close for one week
1944	
Thursday 24 August	Clifton Cinema takes over The *Savoy*
1945	Hudson Cinemas takes over The *Picture House*, Rothwell and renamed The *New Picture House*
1948	
January	Granada Theatres Limited takes over The *Regal* and renames it The *Granada*
September	Northampton Repertory Theatre takes over The *Savoy*
	Hudson Cinemas sells The *New Picture House*, Rothwell to the Rothwell Cinema Company

1950	
April	H. D. Pascoe of Northampton takes over The *Empire*
1951	
Sunday 25 February	The *New Picture House* at Rothwell closes
Monday 24 December	The *Savoy* opens under its own name for stage and cinema
1953	
May	The *Empire* leased to Allcock and renamed The *New Empire*
Wednesday 2 September	The *Gaumont Pavilion* closes for refurbishment
Friday 25 September	and re-opens as The *Gaumont*
1954	
Saturday 19 June	The *New Empire* closes
Monday 4 October	Cinemascope opens at The *Granada* with *The Robe*
1959	
Saturday 3 October	The *Gaumont* closes with *Last Train From Gun Hill*
1960	
Thursday 30 June	The *Ritz*, Desborough closes
Saturday 29 October	The *Odeon* closes with *There Was A Crooked Man*
November	The Watts chain closes The *Electric Palace* at Burton Latimer, The *Regent* at Finedon and The *Picture Drome* at Irthlingborough
1961	
Saturday 25 February	Star Cinemas of Birmingham take over The *Savoy*
Wednesday 8 November	The ex *Odeon* opens as a Bingo hall
1968	
Sunday 25 February	The *Savoy* closes for alteration
April	The *Savoy* Stalls converted to a Bingo Club
Sunday 29 September	The *Savoy* Circle opens as a cinema
1972	
	The ex *Odeon* closes its Bingo hall
1973	
April	The *Savoy* closes for conversion to a twin cinema
Friday 20 April	and re-opens as *Studio 1* and *Studio 2*
1974	
Saturday 8 June	The *Granada* closes
September	The old *Odeon* building demolished

Chronology

1985

Thursday 10 January	The old *Electric Palace*, Burton Latimer reopens as The *Bentley*
Wednesday 24 July	*Studios 1 and 2* close

1986

Easter	*Studios 1 and 2* re-open and renamed The *Ohio*

1996

July	Plans unveiled for multiplex cinema in Kettering under the *Odeon* banner

1997

July	The *Ohio* cinemas close The *Bentley*, Burton Latimer closes
December	A new *Odeon* 8-screen multiplex opens in Pegasus Court, Kettering

INTRODUCTION

When the lights go down...

The murky fog swirled around dimly lit Leicester Square on a March night in 1896. Across the Square from the old Alhambra, the bold, brash musical hall, its rival The *Empire*, was advertising the sensation of the age. The Gothic style building was brightly lit with its four standard globe lamps rising from the balcony above the canopy. Illuminated by three more globe lights, the sign 'Cinematographe Lumieres' was displayed above the entrance.

Within its lovely interior, the full house was awaiting the start of the experience of their lives. They had already heard of the revelation of just two weeks before when in the Grand Hall of the nearby Regent Street Polytechnic the Lumiere Cinematograph show had been presented by Felician Trewy to a paying audience in London for the very first time. And now the audience at The *Empire* could hardly wait to see this new phenomenon of the age – 'living pictures'.

The lights dimmed to just the little gaslights in the aisles, and the audience was hushed in the near darkness as a beam of light from the back of the theatre threw a picture of people outside a factory on to the big screen before them. On the picture, the people moved backwards and forwards, to and fro, and as the images changed constantly, the audience sat with open mouths and with some disbelief at what they were witnessing.

Their eyes had seen, but their minds were unable to take it all in. Some had left, disturbed by the images seemingly rushing towards them from the screen.

Never before had they seen anything like this. It was as if magic powers had been unleashed. The images on the screen could not be heard, but that did not matter, for one miracle at a time was enough.

That occasion was the second public showing of the August and Louis Lumiere 'Cinematographe', and the birth of the cinema in Britain as we know it. The show was destined to run at The *Empire* for fourteen months.

The programmes varied with films of topical and local subjects, many made by British cinematographers, mixed in with firm favourites from the Lumiere brothers. The famous *Empire*, Leicester Square, had become Britain's first cinema.

The Empire*, Leicester Square, London, Britain's first cinema, March 1896, clearly advertising 'The Cinematograph'*

A reporter writing in a popular magazine of the day stated that cinema had arrived, and was an immediate hit. 'To see the carriages roll up outside the Empire would suppose that Leicester Square had only just been discovered. The business is tremendous and there is never a stall to be secured in the evening'.

First to Brighton, followed by Newcastle, cinema spread rapidly across the country. It was a phenomenal success wherever it played, and by December of that year, cinema was established in over 75 cities and towns.

This was quickly followed by the Bioscopes, which travelled the land presenting Animatograph shows at fairs, in halls and even outdoors. The showmen of the day were quick to see the potential of this new and exciting entertainment, and converted sideshows virtually overnight to accommodate the Bioscope, taking the new medium onto the fairgrounds of the country But by 1909, the cinematograph, was going indoors.

This was probably because of legislation for safety, but more, I suspect, because of the all-year-round potential of business opportunity. Halls were being converted, and some purpose-built cinemas established, as well as theatre conversions. So by 1914, the Bioscope had left the fairgrounds and gone into the first cinemas, although many theatres still continued to provide mixed bills of variety and cinematograph.

Kettering's cinema history starts with the showmen, for it was at the fairground on the Recreation Ground, that the 'living pictures' were to make their debut in the town. It is with certainty that the first Bioscope show to a paying audience took place during Feast Week in 1897. The first advertised show to a paying audience seems to have been one given by Mr Warren East at the Victoria Hall in 1901.

In those days advertising was done mainly by handbills and posters and therefore there may have been other shows in public halls such as the Corn Exchange on the Market Place. This venue was showing animated pictures as part of the variety bill from about 1903. The Victoria Hall and the Avenue Theatre booked many touring companies where the Bioscope would be part and parcel of the show.

The cinema as an entertainment in its own right started in 1909 with Vint's Electric Palace in the former Corn Exchange on the Market Place, which remained the major venue for motion picture entertainment until the first propose-built cinema arrived in the form of the Kettering Electric Pavilion on 1913.

Following on, in 1920, was the conversion of the Victoria Hall into the *Victoria Picture House*, and in that year also, The *Empire* was opened in Eskdail Street. The *Avenue* theatre in Russell Street was showing 'living pictures' as well as theatrical presentations, or indeed as part of them, and this was continued when it was converted to the ill-fated *Coliseum*.

In the 1930s, Kettering received its quota of the new palaces of cinema entertainment. The conversion of The *Victoria Picture House* to an *Odeon* was the first modern cinema in the town designed especially for the new 'talkie' pictures, with all the latest technical film presentation equipment. This was followed by the first super-cinema, The *Regal*, which was to become the public's favourite, later being renamed The *Granada*. These palatial cinemas were the essence of comfort and class, and a fitting venue for the ordinary working people of the town to enjoy their hard earned leisure.

With the loss of the old *Coliseum* in 1937, the phoenix-like *Savoy* was the last of the purpose-built cinemas in the town. One little enterprise, however, the cinema in the Working Men's Club, remains a nostalgic memory for many people old enough to remember it.

Around Kettering there were five little cinemas which provided entertainment for their communities, and as such have their place in cinema history. They were The *Electric Picture Palace/Ritz* at Desborough, The *Picture House* (Rowell Pictures) at Rothwell, and then the Watts' chain of cinemas comprising The *Electric Palace* at Burton Latimer, The *Regent* at Finedon and The *Picture Drome* at Irthlingborough.

One by one, these lovely old cinemas have gone, until now we are left with the only cinema in the town, The *Odeon* 8-screen complex which alone carries Kettering's motion picture heritage forward into the new millennium.

In their heyday, the Kettering cinemas provided over 5,000 cinema seats between them, which averaged about one seat for every seven regular picture-goers in the town, and you would be very lucky to find an empty seat on a Saturday evening after 7pm.

This story of the cinemas of Kettering is not a lament to their loss, but a celebration of their existence and of the wonderful medium that was their reason to exist. It is about some of the people who built them, worked in them, and loved them. It is about enterprise and how the working people of a typical town spent some of their leisure, and it is about part of the social history of Kettering.

For those who loved these cinemas, it is hoped the memories of them will be re-kindled. For others too young to have had the cinema experience of yesteryear, I hope this book provides an interesting background to your present day continuing 'movie' experience in Kettering's multiplex.

The 'movies' have been around for a long time – over a hundred years – and the Kettering cinemas are part of that history-

When the lights go down
the screen illuminates with living picture
in a cinema – the temple created for the motion-picture.

PART ONE

THE BIOSCOPES

'Walk up, Walk up to see the pictures that LIVE'. As you walked into the fair on the Recreation Ground, the excitement and bustle that accompanied the Victorian fair engulfed you. The atmosphere was electrifying. The air was filled with that smoky aroma that distinguishes the steam engine smell from any other. The lights were dazzling, and of a magnitude not repeated in between the annual feasts. In the centre of the ground, stood the mighty showmen's engines noiselessly generating the power for the fair, their immaculate liveries matching the beauty of their mechanical excellence.

Around and about, the fair was in full swing. The *Four Abreast Galloping Horses and Ostriches* was fully loaded with punters, screaming with delight, whilst the powering showmen's engine *Emperor* quietly hissed and chugged, oblivious to the antics of its charges.

To the side of the fair, were the many sideshows each providing the 'sensation of the age', from the *Siamese twins and the two-headed snake* to the *Horrors of the Wax Museum*. But the show that stood out from all the rest in this year of 1897, was the new Bioscope, proclaiming the 'latest in living pictures'.

Before its centre steps, the crowd watched with amusement the antics of the troupe of dancers on the boards above, as they danced to the music from the mechanical organ. The 'barker' was enticing the crowd to 'Walk up' and witness the greatest magical show ever – the 'living pictures'. 'See the boxing kangaroo; see the acrobat on a pole, and a visit to the zoo. Thrill to the exotic dancers and the boxing dogs'.

Two pence parted with at the box-office entitled you to crush into the large tent, with rows of benches right down to the small stage on which a large screen was erected. At the rear, was a strange looking machine with a lens, and a bright light in the back. In the dim light the machine whirred as the operator turned the handle, and onto the screen were thrown magical images that moved. The audience responded to every movement and trick on the screen and were both amazed and bewildered. The cinematograph had immediately captured the minds of the Kettering Feast crowds and the cinema had come to town.

William Taylor had converted his sideshow to one of moving pictures in 1897. Previously, his touring show had presented dioramas, but with the success of the cinematograph, like other showmen of his time (the Dooners and the Hancocks, to mention two) Taylor saw the potential pulling power of the new invention, and he began the 1897 season with his Bioscope. He was to bring his show to Kettering for nearly twenty feasts.

Charles Thurston, senior, though a riding master, was also an important developer of the Bioscope. He produced *The Original Royal Show* in 1901 and brought it to Kettering. This Bioscope was a walk-up show with a two-wagon front. In 1909 however, the front was changed to an organ front. The interior was standard tenting with wooden forms as seats. The show had its own attendant engine which was usually the Burrell, number 2462 *Queen Alexandra*, and later the Burrell 2780 *King Edward VII*.

Taylor's Bioscope Show (to the left) and Thurston's Royal Show *side by side at the Recreation Ground fairground site probably around 1902. The picture show shows the* Royal Show *before being converted to an organ front* (D. Wharton)

The 'friendly' rivalry between the two showmen, Taylor and Thurston, saw them trying to outdo each other, which was all the more exciting when, as often, their shows would be next to each other on the fairground. In 1907, Taylor was to bring a larger Bioscope to Kettering. His marquee was said to hold hundreds of people, and with it, he brought his new larger fair-organ the 104 key Marenghi.

The year 1908 saw Charles Thurston present what some people of the day called his greatest achievement, *The Great Show*. It was a combination of Bioscope and vaudeville and was very large in every way. A walk-up show, built by Orton and Spooner, it was very ornate, with carved panels and moulded uprights and was said to be worth walking many miles to see. It had a giant fair-organ, which was a Marenghi from the famous Paris organ builder, with a mammoth 120 key frame. The organ, like the Bioscope, was illuminated by hundreds of small electric lamps which changed colour to the beat of the music (what price the disco outfits of today?). It outplayed anything else on the fair ground and could be heard clearly above the general din. The interior sported velvet seating, tapestry hung walls and was luxury not seen on any fairground elsewhere. It was managed by John H. Norman.

Thurston's Great Show *with its splendid front designed by Orton and Spooner and the 120 Key-frame Marenghi Organ*

On the front stage of *The Great Show*, comics and dancers would perform their crowd-drawing acts. Inside the marquee was a large stage with screen where the 'living pictures' were shown and the vaudeville acts performed. Admission to the show was 3d. The films shown were often repetitions of the previous year's shows, but new items were added of which some would be of local interest. The attendant engines were *King Edward VII, Queen Alexandra*, and the newer Burrell 3075 *Alexandra*.

Records show that in 1907, a device called the 'Chronomegaphone' was included in the Bioscope. This device employed a linking synchronism between a gramophone and the projector, thereby providing sound accompaniment to the pictures. It is not clear whether it was in the Taylor Bioscope or Thurston's, as both seem to have at one time or another presented these first 'sound pictures'. Whilst the device was successful mechanically, it was less than satisfactory because the sound output was no greater than that emitted from an ordinary gramophone horn, thus most of the audience farther back in the show could not hear it.

A typical scene from a short dramatic film which made up a Bioscopic show. One-reelers of about 100 feet or so, they supported 'living pictures' of national and local interest.

The Bioscopes attended the Kettering Feast until 1914, at which time they were taken off the road. The reasons were three-fold. Whilst Taylor and Thurston were very responsible showmen, others were not, and up and down the country serious mishaps in Bioscopes were taking place, particularly with fires, and legislation was brought in to deal with this. Secondly, their popularity was beginning to wane; but lastly, and most importantly, cinemas were going indoors.

Both Taylor and Thurston were pioneers in this field, and met the new challenge by building their own cinemas. Taylor built The *Cinema* at Calne. Thurston built The *Electric Palace* at Harwich, The *Empire* at Biggleswade and The *Cinema Palace* at Norwich. The *Electric Palace* at Harwich still operates to this day.

Thus cinema moved indoors from the hustle and bustle of the fairground and firmed itself as the premier entertainment of that age. The showmanship of William Taylor and Charles Thurston brought the Cinematograph to Kettering and although their visits were only once each year, they provided the very best in moving pictures available at that time.

The fair ground was not the only venue for the Bioscope. Between the years 1901 and 1909, many travelling Bioscope shows visited the town showing either complete film programmes or as part of stage presentations. There were local Bioscope operators also, one notable person being Warren East, who by 1907 had assembled a complete company providing film, music, dialogue and song.

The first recorded 'indoor' Bioscope found so far, was performed at the Oddfellows' Hall, Desborough in December 1897, only months after Taylor's arrival on the Kettering fairground. The visits each Feast and the increasing Bioscope attendance in halls and theatres was providing the demand which was, in 1909, to see Kettering get its first permanent cinema.

PART TWO

THE CINEMAS OF KETTERING

THE CORN EXCHANGE

VINT'S ELECTRIC PALACE

THE PALACE

THE HIPPODROME

The Corn Exchange, one of the remaining buildings of the nineteenth century stands on the Market Square. It has seen many uses and alterations in its time, and for a while, it was the first cinema in the town presenting films and stage presentations.

In 1853 the town was in need of a 'market exchange' and meeting rooms. Kettering was a thriving town and there was also the need for a Town Hall.

Francis Edmund Law of Northampton was required to draw up the designs for a Corn Exchange on the Market Place, and in due course the building was erected for £2,950.

It contained a Market Room on the ground floor, and an upper room which was to serve as the Town Hall. The upper room was on the front of the building over the entrance and offices. The Market Room took up the remainder of the building and had a semi-circular roof, part of which was glazed and supported by cast iron girders. The front of the building was brick built and stone faced with central doors. The building opened in 1854 as the Corn Exchange and Town Hall. At some stage, the Public Library was also housed there.

The main usage was such that during the day it served as the Corn Exchange when required. Other times, and in the evenings, it was used for concerts, lectures, exhibitions, shows and dances. It may have been used for cinematograph presentations prior to 1903, but as no record is available it is not likely, at least for the paying public.

The programme at the Corn Exchange for the week starting Tuesday 10 February 1903 is a particularly interesting one, and is reproduced:

Jasper Redfern presents

THE ELECTRIC DISSOLVING STEREOSCOPE
ANIMATED PICTURES AND ANGLO-AMERICAN VAUDEVILLE
10,000 animated subjects including
THE DELHI DURBAR CELEBRATIONS
THE DENABY COLLIERY EVICTIONS
A TRIP TO THE MOON
ALI BABA AND THE FORTY THIEVES
Plus 20 STAR ARTISTES 20

2/- 1/6d 1/- 6d.
Doors open at 7.30 (Early doors at 7pm 3d. extra)

This programme would have been a touring show, the projector being set up in the hall. The following report of the opening offers some interesting points. Written for the following evening, the *Evening Telegraph* said

> 'the Corn Exchange was well-filled last night when Mr. Jasper Redfern Company gave another splendid entertainment and patrons had an opportunity of seeing the hall alighted with electricity which with its use also saw the illuminating display of his electric dissolving stereoscopic pictures. The photography was supreme and in natural colours well done. (this would refer to *The Trip To The Moon*) Vaudeville entertainment was exceptionally good with Mr. Herbert Betts being a most capable comedian and Mr. W. E. Eel being a cleverly accomplished ventriloquist. The singing of Miss Ada Gray and Mr. Lucien Gray was of a charming description. There should be crowded houses throughout the week right up until Saturday night.'

The Corn Exchange in its earlier days before Vint. It housed the Town Hall and a Library and was always used for public meetings, hustings, concerts and so on

From this report, it seems that Jasper Redfern was known locally thus possibly bringing cinema to the town previously. Electricity had just been installed in the Corn Exchange.

The film *Trip To The Moon* (Mellies, 1902) would have been a 'scoop' for Kettering. In all probability there were more 'animated picture' shows at the Corn Exchange, but in 1909, the building was redundant. A new Corn Exchange had been built in London Road, and a bigger and better Library opened in Sheep Street.

Leo Vint of Long Acre, London, already a cinema owner in those parts, purchased the old Corn Exchange building and gave Kettering its first permanent cinema. He converted the interior and used part of the upper room to construct a balcony. A projection room was constructed to the rear of the balcony, made out of iron sheets. The seating in the rear stalls and the balcony was red plush.

Vint presented both stage turns and pictures twice nightly at 7pm and 9pm, and advertised the acts as being supported by first-class pictures. The prices of admission were 2d, 3d and 6d for the Stalls, and 9d for the Balcony. The General Manager of the theatre was Mr Arthur Brogden. Named as *Vint's Electric Palace*, it opened on the evening of Saturday 16 October 1909, with a programme of variety and pictures presenting American song vocalists Miss St.Malo and Mr Harry Coombes and 'first-class pictures' on the screen.

A newspaper report had this to say:

> 'The immediate success which attended the opening of Vint's Electric Palace was probably unprecedented in the annuls of local entertainment. This new Palace, as most people are aware, is installed in the one-time Corn Exchange and the proprietor and manager have set out with the fixed idea of giving the public what it wants and have been immediately rewarded by the crowded response to the two performances. The sight upon the Market Place was a very unusual one. Brilliantly illuminated the front of the Palace gave a good appearance to the place. A large crowd too was waiting for admittance to the second house before the first had been released and two constables had to be placed at the doors to keep order.
>
> Inside both the splendid furnishings and the excellent programme more than fulfilled the promises made. The old Corn Exchange is quite unrecognisable in its new arraynment every corner of the building being used to its best advantage.
>
> The programmes was a very long one displaying pictures of the most up-to-date kind with songs and dialogues to the films'.

On the façade, the four main buttresses of the building were etched the words COMEDY, DRAMA, TRAVEL and OPERA. During this period, proclamations were often read from the theatre steps, possibly a retainer from the days when the Town Hall was in situ. A photograph of the time shows the proclamation of King George V as King being made there. Interesting to note that in this photograph to the right of the entrance were the Covington's Geisha Tea Rooms, and that there were none of the usual billboards associated with a theatre displayed on the walls.

Leo Vint continued ownership of the theatre until 1912, when John Covington, a Kettering tradesman, leased the property and changed the named to The *Palace*. A private company was formed, known as the Palace Theatre (Kettering) Limited, and registered on Friday 14 June 1912 with a capital of £5,000 in £1 shares. There were two other partners beside Covington, namely Mr G. Foster and Mr T. Johnson. The pictures were advertised as being shown on the 'Palacescope', but it is not recorded as to whether this was the projector or a programme 'presentation'.

After Vint, Covington took over and changed Vint's Electric Palace *to The* Palace. *It retained that name until 1917 when by going over totally to pictures it became The* Hippodrome

During the next two years, The *Palace* was very successful with many famous stars of the stage and screen appearing on its boards. These included Harry Tate, Lilly Langtry, G. H. Elliott, and many others. Pictures were also popular, and one typical programme of Covington's early period was that of the week commencing Wednesday 18 December 1912: 'The Bouncing Dillons', an acrobatic act sharing the bill with the film *A Peep behind the Scenes* (Edison, 1912).

Though no actual dates are recorded it seems that an attempt at 'talking pictures' was made at The *Palace* by placing actors at the rear of the screen to read the dialogue supposedly spoken by the silent stars on the screen. One such drama was *The Bells of Doom*.

By the middle of June 1914, the theatre was in the hands of the Official Receiver, and Covington purchased the rights. He made alterations and re-opened in the August with his two partners, until they left to serve in the Great War.

At the beginning of November 1917, the theatre had changed hands again, this time to Fred Hawkins of Peterborough. The reasons for the changes are obscure, though it might have been that Covington was in financial difficulties. The theatre must have been closed for a short time because on Saturday 3 November, it reopened under Hawkins with a new name, The *Hippodrome*. He had made a number of changes in addition to the name change, the most important being the dropping of stage acts so as to make the showing of films continuous.

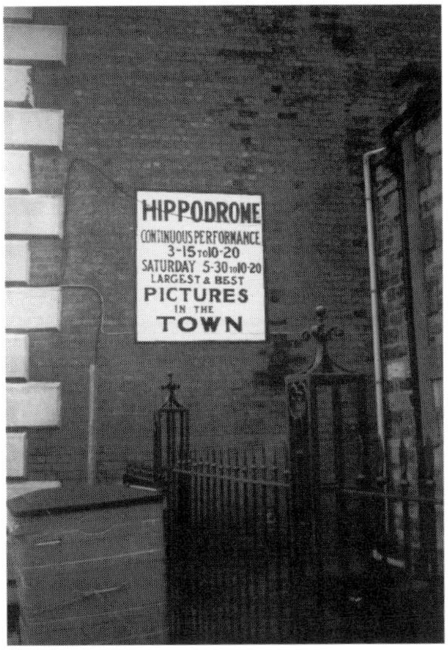

Still existing, and recently restored, the advert for The Hippodrome *painted on the side wall of the building.*

The opening programme however, did include variety acts with a strange, quite odd item under the name of 'Pops Concert Party'. After the opening night, mixed variety and film ceased, and The *Hippodrome* became a full-time cinema, in direct competition as such, with its rival, The *Electric Pavilion*, at the other end of the High Street. Children's shows were run on Saturdays at 2.30pm.

The opening programme is reconstructed from old details:

Mr Fred Hawkins announces the opening of the
KETTERING HIPPODROME
(late VINT'S PALACE)
MONDAY NOVEMBER 3RD. 1917
Continuous Programme 6pm to 10.45pm
VARIETY AND PICTURES + THE BIJOU ORCHESTRA
POPS CONCERT PARTY variety
Pictures SECRETS OF THE SUBMARINE Serial part 1
PEARL OF THE ARMY Pathe Serial Part 1
Starring PEARL WHITE

Seats 2d. 3d. 4d. 6d. and Balcony 1/-

Style of programmes remained almost the same for the next three years until Christmas 1920. After the week starting Monday 27 December the cinema probably did not re-open. The last shows advertised for that week were: Monday to Wednesday *Johnny Get Your Gun* and supporting was *All At Sea.* From Thursday to Saturday was shown *Thirty A Week, Pipe Dreams*, Episode 4 of the Serial *Black Street* starring Pearl White, *Topical Budget*, and the heavyweight championship boxing matches between Beckett and Moran, and Lewis and Basham (yes, really).

There were no further adverts after that week and presumably The *Hippodrome* closed or continued operating without advertised publicity. However, the partnership between Covington, Foster and Johnson was dissolved in June 1922, although Covington is said to have continued the operation until January 1923, when The *Hippodrome* was closed with a formal notice by the Official Receiver.

Part of a Hippodrome *bill advertising* The Kid, *which starred Charles Chaplin and Jackie Coogan, released in 1921. It is unlikely that the* Hippodrome *had a first run of the film. Therefore being a second run, the date may have been Christmas 1921 which meant that The* Hippodrome *continued to show pictures until the business was dissolved in June 1922, solely relying on front of house publicity only.*

After a lengthy receivership case in the courts, a report in the *Kettering Leader* of Friday 9 February 1923 spoke of Covington having debts of £12,921 and described as being a cinema owner and manager. No mention is made of Hawkins.

After further legal proceedings, the judgement was made as expected and was concluded by the statement that the whole affair had been abysmally dragged out and the business lamentable. The dates between the last advertised programme and the Receivership are lacking in reported events and it can either be assumed that programmes did continue with handbills only, or the cinema was actually closed.

Today the building remains and houses a cafeteria and licensed betting shop. Reminders of earlier times can be found on its walls. The words on the buttresses remain after some preservation and on the side wall there is a recently restored advertisement for The *Hippodrome* which pronounces 'continuous performances' and 'the largest & best pictures in the town'.

Projection and technical information

Corn Exchange:
No projection equipment installed. Any film programmes would have been provided by touring Bioscope shows.

Vint's Electric Palace:
The *Palace:*
One Gaumont Chrono Projector, front shutter, with a slide lantern as the light source. Later the light source was improved with either limelight or arc lamp. Power thought to be off the 'mains'.

Hippodrome:
No detail has been found but almost certainly with 'five-reelers' becoming the norm, a second projector would have been installed and probably this was similar to that existing, or as likely newer equipment was installed by Hawkins.

Sometime during the years 1910 to 1918, a Chronomegaphone was installed, but research fails to determine by whom and when. It is possible that Arthur Brogden may have been involved so this would put the period in The *Vint's Electric Palace* days. There was certainly one for a time at The *Hippodrome* for which Fred Hawkins would have been responsible.

THE VICTORIA HALL

THE VICTORIA PICTURE HOUSE

THE ODEON

It has become a part of Kettering – a vein of life-blood of the town'. So it was said of The *Victoria Picture House* when it closed its doors to be modelled into a modern cinema. By that time, the building had served the town for 48 years as a place of entertainment – much of it of excellence. It held a special place in the hearts of theatregoers and cinema fans alike.

The Victoria Hall was to fulfil a need in the town. Apart from the Corn Exchange, public amusement was limited to the two Gaffs in the town, one being a portable theatre erected for travelling shows which became a permanent theatre in Field Street, and later a second one run by a Mr Wild situated in Newland Street. There was no large public hall. The Corn Exchange had only limited seating capacity and the newly formed Kettering Public Hall Company took the opportunity to remedy the need.

Kettering was undergoing rapid changes at this time, and reconstruction was taking place in Gold Street. Cottages, houses and small shops had been pulled down below the site of the Fuller Chapel and a range of new shops were built by the Kettering Post Office Buildings Company. The centrepiece of this development was Kettering Post Office and Arcade. To the west of this new property stood a three-storey mansion which had been the home of Mr Frederick Wallis, one of the founders of the Kettering clothing manufacturers Wallis and Linnell. Mr Wallis died in 1897 and the property came onto the market.

The 3-storey house in Gold Street belonging to Frederick Wallis upon which site the Victoria Hall was built.

The Kettering Public Hall Company saw the opportunity to continue the Gold Street development and purchased the site. They were to sweep away the old house, and construction of the new public hall was commenced by builders Margetts and Neal to design and plans drawn by Messrs Gotch and Saunders. The Hall was to be named the Victoria Hall in recognition of the Golden Jubilee of the reign of Queen Victoria being celebrated at that time.

The new hall was built with a long foyer, the main body of the building well back from Gold Street. The street frontage was of two arches, the right one when facing the building was the public entrance to the auditorium. The other arch was a shop, owned firstly by Horn and Robinson who were piano dealers, then later by the Northamptonshire Printing and Publishing Company, then finally by Thomas H. Day, stationers. Incorporated in the latter was the Victoria Circulating Library. Offices were situated on the first floor.

The official opening date is unclear, but it could have been Sunday 18 December 1888. However, two different newspaper reports record the date as either 1887 or 1889. Considering the time needed to construct such a large development and the reason for its name, it would seem that 1888 would be the most feasible.

Regardless of the doubt about the date, there was no doubt about the success of the grand opening performance of Handel's *Messiah,* followed by a rousing sermon by the then famous atheist orator Charles Bradlaugh. The hall was filled to capacity to hear the Kettering Choral Society enchant those present with spirited and accurate renderings of the famous oratorio to the accompaniment of the orchestra made up of local musicians.

The large stage accommodated the Choral Society comfortably, and the orchestra pit was filled with the musicians. Never before had a Kettering audience seen or heard anything like the sounds that were carried to them buy the excellent acoustic properties which were complimentary to the designers. One wonders at the boldness of the proprietors to follow the great religious work with an oration by Charles Bradlaugh and can only speculate as to how the audience reacted to that.

To the front of the archway which was the public entrance from the street, were two ornate gas-lamp standards their glass displaying the words 'Victoria Hall'. The entrance foyer was long and narrow leading to the auditorium entrance. Inside, a stairway led to the Balcony and Gallery. Two corridors which ran parallel to the auditorium led patrons to the body of the hall. The seating in the Hall was removable and including the Balcony and Gallery could hold between 1,000 and 1,200 people. The interior was tastefully decorated and accommodation very comfortable.

The stage was 55 feet wide and 30 feet deep (about 15 metres by 9 metres). It was equipped with full stage lighting of the day and with four trap doors. There were four dressing rooms back stage and an anteroom which could be used as a kitchen.

The Hall was used for a multitude of purposes. There were, in addition, stage shows, public meetings, bazaars, balls, concerts, opera, and – from time to time – 'animated pictures'. The Hall was also used as a drill hall. Charles Saunders, of Gotch and Saunders, used the Hall for Mission Services and formed the Victoria Mission which later moved to the Tordoff School.

Alf Bailey, noted for his Kettering music business, provided musical accompaniment with his accorded string orchestra. He was to become an important figure with the Hall in the years following.

It would appear that from 1900 the Victoria Hall was presenting stage productions almost constantly and typical of these would be performances of some of the great melodramas of the day. One such example was the play *Star Of Hope* staged by the Miss Wynn Miller Company and presented by the Victoria Theatre Company.

The use of the cinematograph in the Hall is not recorded until March 1901 but the visiting shows were to bring the new medium of cinema regularly, changing in many ways the style of performance which had hither-to been the tradition.

As far as can be determined the first advertised cinematograph show in the Victoria Hall was for the two evenings of Tuesday and Wednesday 12 and 13 March 1901, and in fact may have been the first advertised showing of moving pictures in the town. Mr Warren East was a well-known local businessman and lanternist, and was responsible for the operation and presentation of this show. The publicity was by advert in the *Evening Telegraph* and a reproduction is shown:

THE VICTORIA HALL
KETTERING
Tuesday and Wednesday March 12th & 13th. 1901
Warren East
'LIVING PICTURE' ENTERTAINMENT
War Comic General subjects
Songs by W. Eagle Piano. Mr. Alf Bailey
Pictures include
SCENES AND EVENTS IN THE LIFE OF
H. M. QUEEN VICTORIA
And the complete FUNERAL OF OUR BELOVED QUEEN
Balcony 1/6 Front seats and Gallery 1/- Back seats 6d.

The show was well received as the press report dated Wednesday 13 March shows

> 'Mr. Warren East, the well known; lantern exhibitor, provided a capital cinematograph entertainment for the public in the Victoria Hall which was well filled by a delighted audience. A number of views were first thrown on the screen depicting the splendid manner in which the soldiers have to contend with things in time of [the Boer] War. These were then followed by short films of a number of comic subjects. During a short interval songs were contributed by Mr. W. Eagle and were loudly applauded. Mr, Arthur Turner also merited the recognition of the audience by giving a few selections from the phonograph. Proceeding with the cinematograph entertainment a number of comic pictures were thrown on the screen after which an excellent description was given of the late Queen Victoria's funeral thus enabling those who were deprived of the opportunity of witnessing that historical event to be able to form some idea of the proceedings. A peculiar effect in the final scene is obtained by hundreds of visitors in Hyde Park gradually raising their umbrellas in the falling rain which appears then like a gigantic mushroom forest. Concluding the pictures were views of the mausoleum where the beloved Queen was laid to rest.'

The programme also included the films *Opening Parliament* and *Tour of the Ophir*, plus the English Cup Final (of 1900) together with some local films

Thus the pattern of entertainment at the Victoria Hall was being set for a number of years to come with the insertion of 'film sets' as regular features in shows, in between plays, concerts and even meetings. One such instance was the appearance of 'Poole's Myrioama Combine' including 'Doctor Monnitschew's Wonder Animal Acts'. This was billed for the week starting Sunday 2 February 1902.

'Poole's Myrioama' was a famous travelling show which presented a whole programme of entertainment usually of historical and topical tableaux with music and spoken words. Judging by the newspaper report reproduced below, W. C. Poole had visited Kettering previously, however, not with the cinematograph. Poole would save the films until the last part of the show when with musical accompaniment and oratory from the stage, he would show scenes and events far removed from the staged tableaux for which he was well known.

> 'One of the best variety entertainments which is placed before the public of Kettering is that which is brought at regular intervals to the town by Mr. W. C. Poole. On Monday his company commenced a weeks visit to the Victoria Hall. To say that the large audience was delighted would be but a mild way of expressing their appreciation of the rich treat provided. For fully three hours the interest was maintained and indeed the programme was so immensely varied that to say anyone had experienced a dull moment would be grossly liable.
>
> Mr. Poole's endeavour to make the entertainment attractive was by bringing his splendid pictures up-to-date and his collection of this occasion contained illustrations of the more sterling events in the recent South-African War. Many other striking national events are introduced and there is also a fine series of historical tableaux presenting the battle of Waterloo. The Myrioama is a most agreeably diversified variety of entertainment.'

In 1907 Alf Bailey, involved as Bailey and Company theatrical entrepreneurs, took over the Hall, and it became a theatre. Many famous artistes and theatrical companies were to tread the boards and frequent visits by London companies ensured that Kettering audiences were treated to the great shows of the era, such as *Our Miss Gibbs, The Silver King, The Merry Widow* and *The Arcadians*, to name but a few. Pictures also now were very much part of the presentations and touring cinematograph shows appeared frequently. In 1908 the Hall was advertising the Walturdaw Bioscope Company presenting a programme of films which it is thought included the Pathe *Cinderella* which was a partly coloured film of nearly 1,000 feet in length – an epic of its day.

The Victoria Hall was to spawn many notable local musicians and the orchestra gave regular concerts. Sunday celebrity concerts were held right up until 1920 with famous artistes and military bans featuring. The 1912 Kettering Guide Book quoted '1200 people could see shows with a Balcony having reserved seats at eighteen pence and a Gallery behind at a shilling'.

The Hall had no permanent projection equipment. The films were projected either from the rear of the hall floor or from the rear of the Balcony in a special 'box'. The cinematograph projectors were brought in with the show.

The Victoria Hall closed on the week commencing Monday 5 April 1920 and the final show was a production by Basil Mitchell's London Company of the play *The Lowland Wolf.* The Victoria Hall changed hands with a ceremony on stage on the Saturday evening.

The Hall was to undergo a massive alteration to become a cinema. Work on the conversion was to start immediately under the direction of the newly formed Victoria Company. Shareholding was increased and a number of local dignitaries were elected to the Board. There appears to be no further record of Alf Bailey's involvement.

The conversion involved remodelling the Gallery completely and reconstructing a Balcony with 'raked' seating to give clear views of the stage and screen. The seats were upholstered in crocodile leather and were of the tip-up type. Capacity was reduced to 850 seats. Behind the new Balcony, utilising the old offices and storerooms, the Victoria Tea Rooms were built, although they did not open until some months afterwards.

The projection room was constructed behind the back wall of the stage, thus giving rear projection. The screen was translucent and its surface khaki in colour. It was 'flown' for the purpose of stage presentations. The existing windows were removed and new decorative panels installed giving an elegance to the interior. The exterior was also changed. The two arches were demolished and replaced by a wider entrance and foyer. Over the new entrance a canopy was erected in cast ironwork and glass in a style complimenting the Post Office building's façade. This major reconstruction lasted for four and a half months.

The new cinema, its name The *Victoria Picture House*, opened on Monday 23 August 1920, with a picture which had been released in 1916, *Ragamuffin* starring Mary Pickford. Supporting were *Wild Waves and Women, Ideal Varieties* and a Pathe *Gazette*. The first night was a great success and a welcome was given by the General Manager Arthur E. Melbourne and the Board. The opening programme continued for the first part of a split week and on Thursday changed to *The Common Cause* starring Herbert Rawlinson, again released two years earlier, *Who's With Baby*?, *He's A Devil* and a Pathe *Gazette*.

It is again fortunate that there was a full press report of the first night and although rather long it does describe the new cinema admirably:

> 'Nothing but exclamations of delight and approval was heard at the Victoria Picture House, Kettering on Monday night when the finely appointed cinema opened its doors for the first time and crowd upon crowd of eager folk poured in. Just enough, but no more, of the old Vic remains to emphasise and accentuate the wonderful transformation that has been achieved.

All the windows have gone and in their place are tall panels gracefully decorated with a shade of green and framed in white separating them from other panels of similar design tinged with a delicate buff. Surmounting each panel is a large medallion formed with white fibrous plaster which include a decoration and shaded wall lamps mounted on a pink relief. For the main purposes of illumination electroliers suspended overhead are brought into use the lighting therefore being most pleasant.

The old Vic will be remembered as having a Balcony and Gallery behind. These have been combined so as to form one deeply commodious Balcony every row sufficiently higher than the one before so that one can have an uninterrupted view of the screen and stage. Equally well disposed are the seats in this spacious are. Viewing the Balcony from the floor of the house one gets a particularly pleasing impression of the series of circular mounted plaster-works picked out in white.

After settling down in the seats shown to by the neatly attired usherettes in rose coloured dresses, the audience doubtfully noticed the absence of the overhead 'milky way' on which the pictures travel on their way to the screen from the projector. The explanation is that the astute management has installed special apparatus and the projectors are behind the screen. Every ray of light proceeding from the machine goes directly onto the screen, whilst on the other hand it has not been necessary to throw the auditorium into quite the dense Egyptian darkness as one usually associates with picture shows.

It is good to note that Mr. White, the operator, rendered a like service to the troops in France and it is admirable to also note that every male member of the staff is an ex-serviceman. Mondays two programmes proved right worthy occasions and following the opening comments by dignitaries the film of Pathe scenes were shown by thrilling mountaineering pictures and the film "Ragamuffin", a six part production in which the universally popular Mary Pickford made many more friends. Finally "Wild Waves and Women", a comedy, had the whole house in a roar. Mrs. Melbourne, the musical director, made delightful use of the upright grand piano supplied by Alf Bailey.'

THE VICTORIA PICTURE HOUSE,
GOLD STREET, KETTERING.
General Manager ... ... ARTHUR E. MELBORNE.
MONDAY, TUESDAY & WEDNESDAY, August 23rd, 24th and 25th,
MARY PICKFORD in
:: THE RAGAMUFFIN. ::
A World's Favourite Artiste in a Picture which stands alone.
Wild Waves & Women, a Sunshine Comedy. Ideal Varieties. Pathe Gazette.
THURSDAY, FRIDAY & SATURDAY, August 26th, 27th and 28th,
One of the Greatest Pictures of the Year:
THE COMMON CAUSE,
A Vitagraph Drama of Intense Interest. "I don't like it, so don't do it."
Who's With the Baby, Comedy. He's a Devil. Pathe Gazette.
MATINEE FRIDAY at 2-30. EVENINGS: Doors open 6 o'clock. Continuous Performance 6.15 to 10.30
Admission: 6d., 9d., 1/-. Balcony 1/6. Reserved 2/-. Tax included.
— ORCHESTRA. —
Tip-up Seats throughout by Bobby, Ltd., Bournemouth. LUNCHEON. TEA and SUPPER ROOMS will be opened as soon as Alterations are completed.

A newspaper advert for the opening week of the Victoria Picture House *in August 1920*

The *Victoria Picture House* did not however abandon stage productions. The excellent stage of the old Victoria Hall had been preserved in the alterations and for many years the Kettering Operatic Society was to present its shows here. There were also the occasional stage shows and concerts, but it was most certainly first and foremost a cinema.

In the beginning, the musical accompaniment to the films was the upright grand piano with Mrs. Melbourne at the keys. Shortly after the opening of the cinema, she was leading a quartet and in 1926 there was a sextet led by Maurice Friedman who was to become an accomplished local musician in his own right. In 1928 the cinema had the full orchestra of ten musicians led by another well-known local musician, John Sugden. So good was this orchestra that it played musical interludes during intermissions and between films.

During its life, The '*Vic*' as the public continued to call it, saw the advent of the 'talkies'. Contrary to expectation, The '*Vic*' was to be the first to show 'talkies'. The first sound film shown, according to adverts, was in the programme for the week commencing Sunday 9 June 1929 when the short *Cavaleria Rusticana* featuring the Celeste Octet was shown, followed by a film extract dramatised by Bransby Williams from Charles Dickens' *Bleak House* called *The Characterisation of Grandfather Smallwood.*

Looking down Gold Street in the 1930s, the Post Office buildings are to the right and the sign PICTURES is visible on the Victoria Picture House (Evening Telegraph)

Later, from Monday to Wednesday 1 to 3 July 1929, a famous stage figure of the time, Ernest Latinga starred in *The Raw Recruit* which was a short featuring his well-known stage scena. The following week George Robey was to be seen in a 'talkie' *The Barrister*. A report in the *Evening Telegraph* confirms these showings in this extract from a review of the films of the week:

> 'The talkie showing this week at the Victoria Picture House featuring Ernest Latinga in his hilarious sketch "Raw Recruit" seems to rectify the chief fault that Kettering audiences have found in the talkies and that is lack of action.'

Thus it would appear that The *Vic* was showing 'talkies' as early as June 1929, six months before The *Electric Pavilion* was to show its fist 'talkie', though the newspaper report suggests there had been earlier 'talkie' shows. As no other adverts or reports appear before the show of Sunday 9 June 1929 it must stand as the first 'talkie' in the town. There is some confusion as to when and what sound equipment was installed, but in 1929 a British Talking Picture sound system was in situ and the films described may have been using the sound-on-disc system.

Looking in the opposite direction, early 1920s (D. Wharton)

Much of the programme content was still silent however, and some of the greatest silent films of the era played at The '*Vic*'. It was styled as the best picture palace in town and indeed it was, with its flush furnishings and atmosphere of 'class'. It is said that its Balcony was one of the finest examples around and matched anything to be found in Northampton or Leicester, and all of this for just 6d, 9d and 1s in the Stalls and 1s 6d (2s reserved) in the Balcony.

The *Victoria Picture House* was to continue its business into the 1930s, eventually, like its competitors, presenting 'talkies' to the ever increasing audiences. For myself I can only dimly remember the entrance, and unfortunately very little of the inside save the long foyer in which I am sure there were display windows for shops. I do remember a poster front of house advertising the film for the week of closure, and that was *Come Out Of The Pantry*, and although one of my aunts would often take me to the pictures after school (I was seven then) I cannot remember if she obliged on that occasion.

The Victoria Picture House *entrance. The billboard advertises the film* The White Cockatoo *which dates this picture to early 1936, only months before The 'Vic' was rebuilt as The* Odeon

The *Victoria Picture House* closed with the last performance on Saturday 24 April 1936. It was not without some sadness, and although a new modern cinema was to be built from The '*Vic*', this report from the *Kettering Leader* at the time best sums up the local feelings:

> 'Losing and old friend.
>
> On Saturday night the owners of the Victoria Picture House closed their doors on a past of entertainment and social activity as one of the oldest public halls in the town. The Vic, dear to the hearts of many because of its many memories they have for it, has had a long career. It has become part of Kettering, a vein of life blood of the town and it is not without a sigh or regret that it now closes its doors as the Vic forever.'

The *Odeon* was constructed from the shell of the closed *Victoria Picture House*. On Thursday 16 January 1936 the new Odeon (Kettering) Limited company took over the old picture house and closed it after the last show on Saturday 24 April 1936 for reconstruction.

Odeon (Kettering) Limited was a subsidiary of Odeon Theatres Limited headed by the cinema entrepreneur Birmingham based Oscar Deutsch. By that time, his empire was expanding rapidly with over 200 cinemas nationwide. The sum involved in the take-over was about £50,000, of which £15,000 was set aside for the massive alterations needed.

The shareholders of the old Victoria Company were paid £1 5s for each £1 share they had (a 25% appreciation) of which 65% was paid in cash with the remainder given in shares in the new company. Thus the shareholders of the Victoria Company became shareholders in Odeon (Kettering) Limited.

Work to transform the old building began immediately after the closure. The Balcony was completely dismantled and a new 'Circle' erected. A new projection room was constructed in part of what had been the Tea Rooms behind the Balcony and the old projection area back stage removed.

The street front was completely swept away, breaking architectural unity with that side of Gold Street. In its place was constructed an ultra-modern frontage with tinted green, white and black tiling. Added was a modern canopy with letterbox and a fin above with the letters ODEON on both fascias. Above the canopy was a large 36 pane decorative window, illuminated at night. High above, striped tiling decorated the upper part of the front and side, and a large neon-lit ODEON sign was displayed on the side face of the building. It was a very imposing frontage and quite beautiful in its way giving a very modern look to Gold Street even though it broke with conformity.

The Odeon, *Gold Street. This picture was taken towards its final years as a cinema. After some years as a Bingo hall it was demolished in 1974* (T. Smith)

The entrance was full width leading to two sets of doors. Inside was a foyer containing a central pay desk, sales kiosk and display area. The old corridor entrance to the stalls was blocked off and a new entrance into a holding area was constructed. Two sets of doors led left and right into the Stalls. The circle was gained by stairs to the left of the entrance foyer, and these led to what was known as a 'crush area' where patrons queuing for Circle seats could be held. Before the Second World War part of this are was used as a café. Entry to the Circle was by side entrances from another small foyer which also held washroom facilities. And the door to the projection room.

The seating was increased to 740 in the Stalls and 350 in the Circle, although other figures suggest that the total seating may have been 1250. The interior décor was also of ultra-modern lines with a central plasterwork extrusion running full length of the ceiling which housed the main lighting. A similar plasterwork feature ran from the proscenium each side at the same level, meeting up with the circle. This was also a source of the main lighting. The proscenium was also of a concave design patterned with 'sound and air' apertures and was decoratively lit.

Records do not show whether or not the stage was removed. Some reports of the day suggest that it was planned to remove it. However in the new cinema there was a substantial stage are and also an orchestra pit so modifications may well have been made to the original stage. The dressing rooms however, were retained.

The screen was towards the back wall with a sound chamber behind. The most unusual feature of the cinema was the great maroon stage tabs (curtains) and behind them the beautiful silk screen tabs with an embroidered scene of butterflies and flowers. It was a beautiful piece of work.

The main colour scheme throughout the cinema was predominantly shades of buff matched with doors of maroon with other features picked out in cream and black. A later decoration about 1951 provided a colour scheme of shaded pinks with black doors outlined in cream. The *Odeon* was Kettering's first 'super cinema' and an ultra-modern delight, and the cinema going public took to it at once.

The cinema opened on Saturday 19 September 1936. On stage were the local dignitaries, and the opening ceremony was performed by Mr Steven Schilizzi, MP. There then followed a prelude by Harry Pell's Premiers band. The film programme began with a cartoon *Robber Kitten*, followed by Universal *Talking News* and the feature *Strike Me Pink* (1935) starring Eddie Cantor. The cinema foyer was ablaze with baskets of chrysanthemums and drapery. Seats had been booked solid for days before the opening.

Of the cinemas in the town that offered Saturday children's matinees, perhaps The *Odeon* is the best remembered. I cannot recall whether it was the first to do so, but it was certainly the best, at least, that is what the kids thought in those days, after all, who else was showing *Flash Gordon* serials? The *Odeon* Club Song was reverently chanted every Saturday to a level that could be heard outdoors, such was the fervour of the 740 kids in the stalls.

Every Saturday morning where do we go?
Getting up to mischief? Oh dear no!
To the Mickey Mouse Club
With our badges on
Every Saturday morning at The *Odeon*.

The imposing front of The Odeon *in its prime* (Evening Telegraph)

The *Odeon* was to remain a popular cinema throughout its life. It was comfortable and luxurious. In 1954 a wide screen was installed and was equipped with new projectors. The Rank Organisation, which owned The *Odeon*, shunned the new Cinemascope format at first, because Twentieth Century Fox, whose process it was, insisted that full magnetic stereophonic sound equipment be installed as well.

The result was that The *Odeon* lost the films from the Fox distributors for a while. Fortunately at the time however, Paramount brought out a new process called VistaVision which required no major installation. Thus The *Odeon* was able to continue to present the latest films. A little while later, however, Cinemascope became available without the stereophonic sound system being necessary, and so the *Odeon* was able to screen the Fox films again.

From time to time concerts would be staged, but The Odeon was foremost a cinema and many of the greatest films ever made were portrayed on its screen. There was even a world premier when the cinema presented a charity showing of *The Browning Version* (see part 4).

The *Odeon* had numerous managers during its life, with each one contributing much to the cinema's success. Cooke, Shepheard, Brett and Barlow to name but a few, but none more so than Bert Dawson who was the essence of a cinema manager and of whom I shall refer to later in the book.

"Starry night for the Odeon *usherettes. Actress Marjorie Rhodes gets a warm greeting from the staff of the* Odeon *Cinema at Kettering. The year was 1953 and Marjorie was in Kettering to help with the publicity for* Decameron Nights *in which she starred with Louis Jourdan, Joan Fontaine and Joan Collins. The actress had been invited to the* Odeon *by manager John Barry".*

My recollections of The *Odeon* are of its class and comfort. It obviously followed the standards set up by its predecessor. Again, with my aunt, I remember going to The *Odeon* to see *Pennies From Heaven* (1936) starring Bing Crosby. As I recall, my aunt was mad about the popular crooner, hence the visit. I remember little of the film but I do recall entering the cinema for the first time, and the memory of the warmth of it which was to remain with me into adulthood. It always seemed different to other cinemas. They all had their own 'feel', but The *Odeon* was class. If you went to a matinee, I recall, you would receive twenty minutes or so of Victor Sylvester records playing the tunes of the day. When I hear his music occasionally nowadays, my thoughts always go back to the days of those matinees at The *Odeon*. I often wonder whether the recordings were a favourite of Lance Roberts, Bert Dawson or even Oscar Deutsch himself.

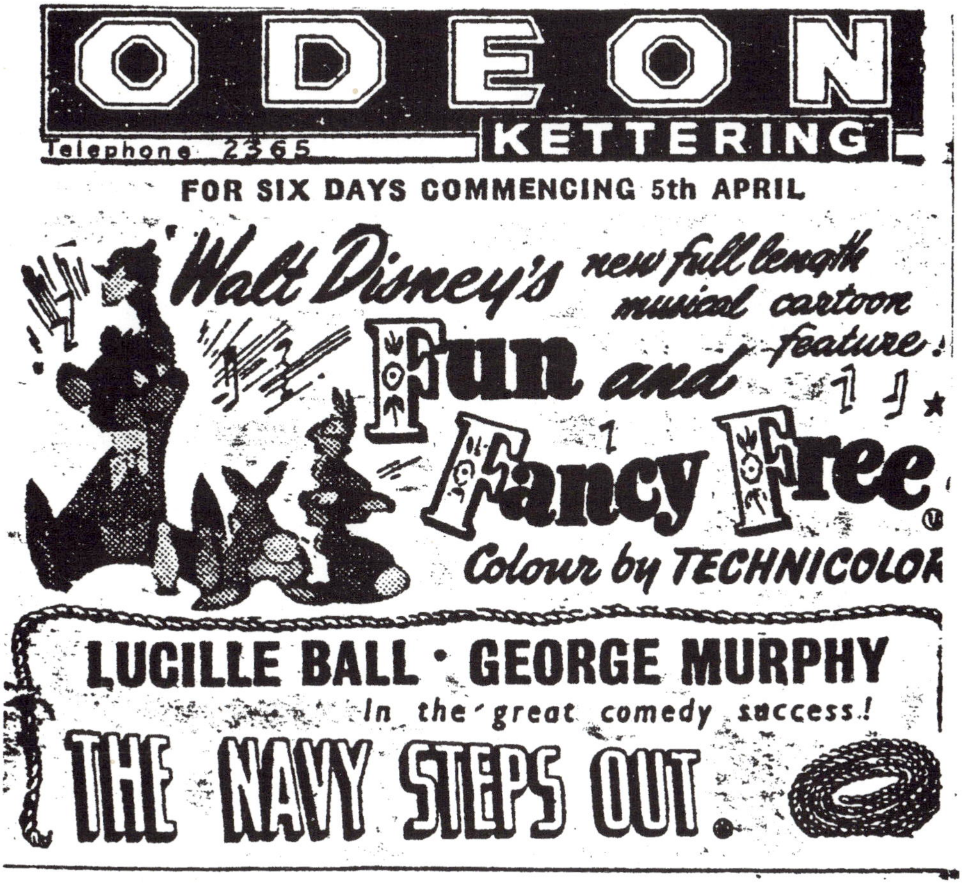

Typical newspaper publicity for The Odeon, *1947* (Evening Telegraph)

It was always a busy cinema, especially on a Saturday night. Even to be sure of getting in for the last performance, usually about 7.20pm, one would need to join the queue, threading its ways down Bakehouse Hill, by 6pm. The doorman walked miles, for he traversed the queue constantly, which often stretched beyond the Peacock on the opposite side of Lower Street, calling for singles or doubles as they became available during the continuous performances.

The name's Bond – Derek Bond. A publicity 'blurb' featuring the British film actor Derek Bond on a visit to The Odeon*, early 1950s*

Little wonder then, that the announcement to close The *Odeon* was met with dismay in the town. True, the cinema suffered with the cinema-going decline, but it was still popular. The final week, the film showing was *There Was A Crooked Man* starring Norman Wisdom. How fitting that the last film was a comedy, for it was a comedy film with which it had opened.

On Saturday 29 October 1960, The *Odeon* closed its doors as a cinema for the last time, and 72 years of entertainment on the site was finished; though not quite, for after 14 months of closure, the building was re-opened as a Bingo hall. This was not particularly successful but it remained as such for a little over ten years before finally closing in 1972. The building remained boarded up until September 1974 at which time it was demolished to make way for what is now part of the Newborough Centre.

I remember at the time that there was much opposition to its fate by townspeople, and many wanted to see it taken up by the Council and used as a Civic Theatre, but alas the faint heart lost the fair lady and the old *Odeon* was to go forever.

Projection and technical information

Victoria Hall:

The cinematograph projection equipment would have been supplied by the Bioscope shows, and in the instance of Warren East, by himself. Invariably the cinematographs would have been virtually any make, from Cinematographe's to those made and supplied by Acres, Paul and other British makers. Unfortunately no records exist for accurate details. The screen seemingly was 'flown' or rolled up.

Victoria Picture House:

The projection room was behind the stage wall and the screen was likely 'flown'. It was a translucent rear projection screen, somewhat khaki in colour to look at, but the pictures apparently were superb. The projectors installed until 1928 were two mute Kalee 7s. British Talking Picture sound heads were installed in 1928 with the same company installing the amplification equipment. Here there is some controversy because whilst it is quite possible sound-on-film equipment was available, some of the early shorts shown at The '*Vic*' were sound-on-disc which would suggest that the usual Vitaphone disc reproduction equipment would have been installed early in 1929, or even late 1928, and at the rear of the Kalee 7s. However, other 'shorts' are known to be in the Movietone sound-on-film system also. It is fairly safe to assume that The '*Vic*' was equipped only for sound-on-disc. The first of such films *The Jazz Singer*, does not appear to have been shown, as this was never advertised.

The projection room had a slide projector, and the speaker system, seemingly, was through the outlets around the proscenium. It is possible that new projection equipment was installed about 1931 and this would have included a sound-on-film system, as there exists an application in the Records Office to install sound equipment. Unfortunately there are no records of details, but this being the case, the cinema was either late in transferring to sound-on-film, or was updating equipment.

The *Odeon:*

The projection room was removed from its position back stage in The *Victoria Picture House* to a new room behind the Circle. It was equipped with two British Thomas-Houston (BTH) projectors fitted with BTH sound heads. The amplification was also BTH. Speakers were mounted behind the perforated screen in a special sound chamber back stage.

About 1954 the two projectors were replaced with Kalee 21s. It is not clear whether the sound system was also changed but I seem to remember seeing

Western Electric amplifier racks on my visits to the projection room in the mid 1950s. Projectormatic was also installed. To accommodate the ratios of the new film processes, Delrama anamorphic lenses were fitted to the Kalee 21s.

In 1936 when The *Odeon* opened, the screen was a standard Academy ratio of 1:33 to 1. Possibly in the years between 1936 and 1954 there may have been a replacement screen, but in 1954 a new screen was installed, being a multi ratio screen with variable masking, making possible aspect ratios from the standard wide-screen format of 1:75 to 1 out to Cinemascope, 2:35 to 1, thus enabling 35mm VistaVision optical Cinemascope and numerous derivative systems to be accommodated.

The projection room also contained the usual still projection equipment and lighting controls for stage and auditorium and well as the non-sync. It is believed that this final set-up remained until closure.

THE
AVENUE

THE
COLISEUM

THE
NEW COLISEUM

THE
SAVOY

STUDIOS 1 and 2

THE
OHIO

'The towns-people were not slow in showing their delight at having a comfortable theatre'. That comment from a newspaper report was made at the opening of Kettering's newest theatre, The *Avenue* in 1902. But it was Thomas Payne who had opened the first theatre, a 'gaff' in the town, a few years earlier.

At first it was a portable theatre erected for visiting shows. Later a permanent theatre was erected by him in Field Street, and became known as the 'penny gaff'. Thomas Payne had two sons, William and Frank. William (of W.J. Payne, Builders) had acquired land in Russell Street to build houses, and had laid the foundations. It was early in 1902, and the theatrical activities at the Victoria Hall had put paid to the 'penny gaff'. Instead of the houses, the brothers decided to build a permanent theatre, with the sole proprietor being Frank Payne.

It was a fine theatre for a town the size of Kettering, and in those days, unlike the Victoria Hall, was designed and built for the express purpose of providing stage presentations. It was however, quite a strange design. The auditorium was built parallel to Russell Street which required a vast wall running the length of the building down the street. This wall was not particularly attractive but it proved to be a blessing later on in the theatre's life. The entrance was not on the street, but via an opening, leading off the street at the west end. Mention is made in David Bradshaw's descriptive article *My Technicolor Boulevard* of two large wooden gates, not unlike factory gates, being across the access. It is possible that these were pit in place when the *Avenue* theatre was built. It gave the street perspective of the building as being somewhat like a factory, but this was soon dispelled as soon as one entered the building.

The entrance foyer contained the pay-box, each side of which a set of stairs took patrons to the Balcony. Beyond the pay-box was a wide corridor on the left side of the building (next to, and parallel to, Russell Street) which ran the length of the auditorium. From this corridor, access to the Stalls was made through sets of doors. The seating was comfortable, those in the balcony were priced at 6d for covered, and 9d for the plush seats. The Stalls were 2d, 4d, 6d, and 9d with seats ranging from plush upholstery to no upholstery at all. The seating capacity was about 800.

The stage was large, measuring some 22 feet wide, 20 feet high and 30 feet deep (approximately 7 x 6.5 x 9.5 metres). The proscenium was constructed mostly of wood and canvas with the latest electric stage lighting. The drop curtain was of a Northumbrian castle scene.

The theatre was filled to capacity on the opening night of Bank Holiday Monday 3 August 1903, with dignitaries taking all the 'posh' seats at the front poof the Stalls and the Balcony. Every seat in the house was taken for the opening show which was to be one of the most outstanding if its kind, and of the likes never seen in Kettering before. Opening a week of opera, the Neilson English Grand Opera Company performed Gounod's *Faust* to resounding applause from the audience who joined in the popular choruses during the finale of the opera. The same was to be repeated throughout the week of popular opera presentations.

NEW AVENUE THEATRE
Russell Street Prop. F. Payne
GRAND OPENING
Bank Holiday Monday, August 3rd. 1903
The NEILSON ENGLISH GRAND OPERA COMPANY
FAUST

Tuesday August 4th	MARITANA
Wednesday August 5th	LILLY OF KILLARNEY
Thursday August 6th	TANNHAUSER
Friday August 7th	IL TROVATORE
Saturday August 9th	DAUGHTER OF THE REGIMENT

Seats STALLS 2d 4d 6d 9d   BALCONY 6d & 9d

The report in the following evening's paper was full of praise for the new theatre

'Opening of the Avenue Theatre

Amid every sign of enthusiasm for its future successes the curtain was rung up for the first time on the stage of the New Avenue Theatre in Kettering last night when a capital performance of 'Faust' was given by the Neilson English Grand Opera Company. There were many evidences that Kettering residents were alive to the fact that Monday evening would see the making of history so far as theatrical enterprise in the town was concerned. It is not therefore surprising that there was an overflowing audience besieging the theatre with an expectation that was fully justified.

> The interior of the theatre presents a cosy appearance, the comfortable stalls being occupied by the prominent townspeople who were not slow in making their appreciation in having a comfortable theatre in their midst. The effective drop scene painted by Mr. A. Maude depicting Alnwick Castle was duly admired and the orchestra, having tuned up, the said curtain rose on to full company of artistes who were ready to perform.
>
> The orchestra struck up the National Anthem and a few minutes later the curtain rose again to find Faust mourning his lost youth and the opening scene of Gounod's most famous opera was in full swing.'

The theatre showings of 'animated pictures' are obscure, although there was an advertisement for a week in September 1908 when the 'St Lawrence Picture Co' was booked in. The theatre relied upon visiting Bioscopes and had no cinematograph equipment installed. Projection was set up at the rear of the Stalls by the visiting Bioscopes.

In November 1908, the theatre closed and was opened up as a skating rink by a business syndicate named the Kettering Rink Company. It was not a great success however and lasted just two years as a Rollerdrome. In November 1910, things were to change.

> 'Have you seen the pictures and variety at the Kettering *Coliseum*. This week they are good. Next week they will be better. Our pictures cannot be beaten – equalled – but not beaten'.

So ran the challenge in the advertisement for the week of Monday 7 November 1910. After the unsuccessful skating rink venture, the premises re-opened as a theatre for variety and pictures. It had a new name. The *Coliseum*.

During the twenty three months as a skating rink, picture entertainment in the town had taken off with outstanding popularity. The Victoria Hall was providing plays and 'living pictures' on a regular basis. Leo Vint had opened his *Palace* with the popular manager Arthur Brogden in charge and with The Avenue no longer in competition with variety entertainment, he had full rein. Pictures were an important part of the programme at *Vint's Electric Palace*. The *Palace* was not a large venue and there was room for an enterprise of a similar nature, and so with new lessees and a new name, The *Coliseum* was about to do battle and take the ground. That challenge in the opening week advertisement fired the first salvo.

The theatre had been leased to Jack Maynard and O. P. Drever, Junior. The first General Manager was William Jackman, who in service during the Boer War had been mentioned in despatches for rescuing his sergeant under fire after the man had been seriously wounded. With this background as his spur, he made some dramatic changes to the theatre.

The interior was completely re-decorated and re-seated throughout with plush tip-up seats. The stage was rebuilt and had splendid painted scenery and proscenium decoration. A projection box was installed in the rear Stalls and lined with asbestos. In this box was installed one projector with which one-reel films were shown. The outside of the theatre was enhanced with powerful electric lighting making a very cheerful appearance. A report in the *Evening Telegraph* perhaps describes the change more significantly, under a heading 'Pictures and Song', and dated Thursday 10 November 1910.

> 'The Avenue Theatre in Russell Street has suffered many vicissitudes during its years of existence but it seems now to have permanently disappeared in that character and re-appeared under the guise of the Kettering Coliseum, a picture palace of the most up-to-date kind.'

Jackman employed a full orchestra to accompany the singing and dancing, to play interludes and to the pictures, an improvement, it was said, on the lone piano. He provided popular and high-class variety and he personally picked the films shown. This was noted in a report of the opening night that

> 'films picked by Mr. Jackman include some of the most beautiful coloured pictures besides a complete range of interesting stories which are thrown on to the screen by one of the most powerful electric machines made and which shows practically no flicker at all.'

The opening night was on Monday 7 November 1910 with a programme including 'All the Latest Pictures and Variety'. No details were reported. However, the programme for the following week variety included 'The Maximillian Trio' (jugglers), Alexander Mee (special song scena) and 'Carrie and Moore' (American comedians and soft-shoe dancers). Supporting were

'All the Latest Pictures'. Seat prices were Pit 3d, Back Pit 2d, Orchestra Stalls 6d, Balcony 6d. Business was excellent with full houses at most performances.

The film performances were usually one-reelers which were shown in between the various actsion the stage. Most pictures ran about ten minutes or so and the story (if any) would be told within that one reel. About that time films were being produced that were longer, two-reelers, or more, and were beginning to make their presence felt in the mixed stage and film programmes. They were shown separately as a film in two parts, three parts, and soon.

By the spring of 1911, the theatre had changed hands again. The brothers Arthur and James Thompson were to take over the business, with Arthur being the General Manager. There is nothing recorded to indicate what happened to the former lessees or to Jackman for that matter. Mr Wilfred G. Sturman was appointed musical director of the pit orchestra at the same time.

The operation of The *Coliseum* continued in much the same pattern for the following years. It is thought that an additional projector was installed enabling longer films to be shown, but the building remained very much a theatre and throughout the years many famous stars were to tread its boards, including Harry Tate, 'Buffalo Bill' Cody, Gracie Fields (billed as Miss Grace Field) and many more. The boast of having the best pictures was progressively delivered as was evident for the week beginning Tuesday 12 December 1912 when the theatre was advertising 'all the latest pictures on the silver screen'.

One interesting programme is that for the week beginning Friday 14 June 1912 when on stage was billed 'Atlas and Vulcana' – the most graceful athletes and the strongest lady living. Pictures on the silver screen included *The Strange Adventures of Tom Butler* and *The Derby 1912*. There would seem to have been a spate of such acts locally, for that very same week *Vint's Electric Palace* was advertising *Whizzing the Whirl*, sporting novelty acts and the latest pictures, including *The Derby 1912*.

The Thompson brothers were to remain the lessees for many years, but towards the latter part of the 1920s The *Coliseum* was experiencing difficulties and there were spasmodic closings and re-openings. In the latter part of 1928 the death of Frank Payne, described as the owner and builder, occurred, and it is supposed that this was the reason for the closure of the week of Monday 10 December. The usual advertisement of the entertainment page of the *Evening Telegraph* stated that for the week of Monday 17 December the theatre was closed, 'owing to a disappointment'. For the week Tuesday 2 July 1929, a similar advertisement appeared again with no apparent reason given.

With the death of Frank Payne, The *Coliseum* was put up for sale by auction. From a newspaper report, this time from the *Kettering Leader* dated Friday 31 May 1929, it is clear that the theatre was experiencing a difficult time.

> **'Kettering Coliseum reserve price not reached.**
>
> The reserve price of the Kettering Coliseum was withdrawn at £2, 950 when offered for sale by auction at the Royal Hotel. The sale was due to the death of the owner Mr. Frank Payne who built the theatre in 1903. About twenty people were present. The first offer was for one thousand five hundred pounds and the amount rose steadily by one hundred pound bids to two thousand nine hundred pounds. An advance of fifty pounds was secured and at this stage the auctioneer announced that he must withdraw the property. The theatre holds 850 people and is let at two hundred and fifty pounds per year to Messrs Thompson Brothers who have the option of continuing their tenancy until 1934.'

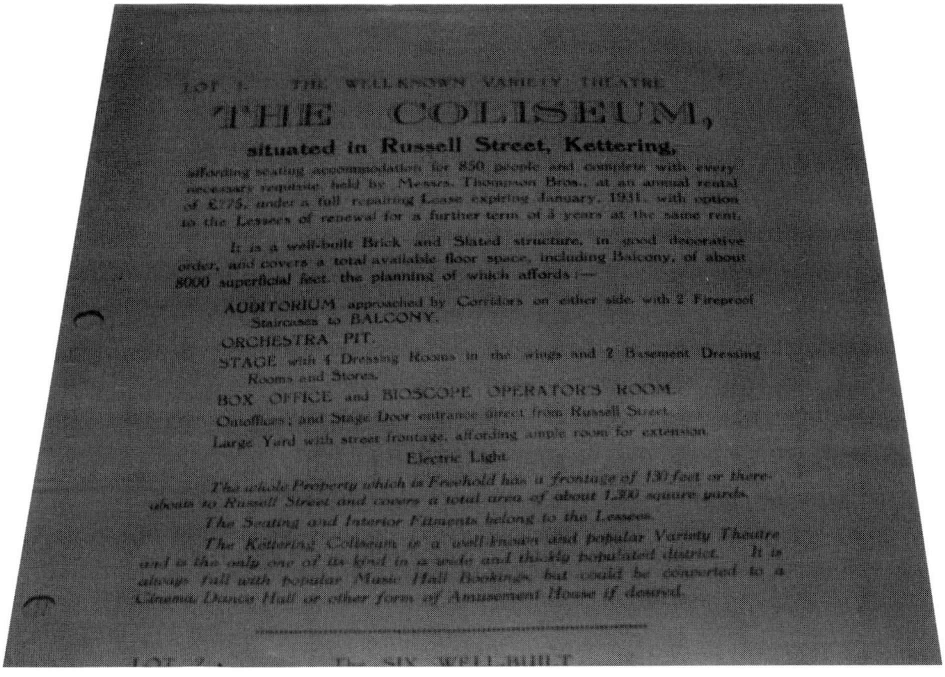

LOT 1. THE WELL-KNOWN VARIETY THEATRE

THE COLISEUM,

situated in Russell Street, Kettering,

affording seating accommodation for 850 people and complete with every necessary requisite, held by Messrs. Thompson Bros., at an annual rental of £275, under a full repairing Lease expiring January, 1931, with option to the Lessees of renewal for a further term of 3 years at the same rent.

It is a well-built Brick and Slated structure, in good decorative order, and covers a total available floor space, including Balcony, of about 8000 superficial feet, the planning of which affords:—

AUDITORIUM approached by Corridors on either side, with 2 Fireproof Staircases to BALCONY.

ORCHESTRA PIT.

STAGE with 4 Dressing Rooms in the wings and 2 Basement Dressing Rooms and Stores.

BOX OFFICE and BIOSCOPE OPERATOR'S ROOM.

Outoffices; and Stage Door entrance direct from Russell Street.

Large Yard with street frontage, affording ample room for extension.

Electric Light.

The whole Property which is Freehold has a frontage of 130 feet or thereabouts to Russell Street and covers a total area of about 1,200 square yards.

The Seating and Interior Fitments belong to the Lessees.

The Kettering Coliseum is a well-known and popular Variety Theatre and is the only one of its kind in a wide and thickly populated district. It is always full with popular Music Hall Bookings but could be converted to a Cinema, Dance Hall or other form of Amusement House if desired.

The item in the prospectus for the sale of The Coliseum *in May 1929, at which the reserve price of £2,950 was not reached*

The fortunes of The *Coliseum* from 1929 seem unclear. Apart from the closure in July 1929 for a short season, programmes of stage performances continued. An interesting anecdote concerns the week of Monday 17 February 1930 when the theatre was advertising *Blackmail* with the rider 'a play in three acts. Not the talkie, but the REAL thing'.

The last Managing Director the theatre had was a certain Jack Sherwood who hailed from Tipton in Staffordshire and who had married May, the daughter of Frank Payne. On Friday 7 August 1931 he took over control of The *Coliseum*. The circumstances under which this came about are unknown, but he was to make some important changes to the old theatre.

The *Coliseum*, and The *Avenue* before it, was listed as a Music Hall. It was never really, and the new director was to dispel that misnomer for all time. Within a year Sherwood had removed the old projection box from the rear Stalls and built a new one behind the Balcony wall. New projection equipment was installed and the building was wired for sound. Seating was renewed throughout with pink plush tip-up seats. The interior was changed by upgrading the entrance and access to the auditorium. He gave it another name, The *New Coliseum*, and set the prices of admission at 6d, 9d and 1s for the Stalls, and 1s 6d for the Balcony.

Changes to the theatre continued piecemeal and new stage lighting and fittings were installed. New draperies were fitted, and the improvements were continually visible to the delighted patrons on their visits. It opened under its new name on Wednesday 3 August 1932 with, oddly, a play *Bird in Hand.*

Jack and May Sherwood became popular figures about the town. Sherwood was to bring many fine acts to the stage and these were interspersed with popular films of the day showing in their own right with the latest equipment. The Manager was Harold Jackson, who was a 'matinee idol' type, totally suitable to the role he was to play in the theatre's success.

So it was then that The *New Coliseum* enjoyed popularity as an entertainment venue in the town under the dynamic new management. Stars of the stage and radio were to appear on its vast stage, and on its screen the latest pictures and film stars of the day appeared, to delight the patrons. However, on Tuesday 6 April 1937, the greatest drama ever to be played out at the old theatre was to take place.

It was about 4am on that fateful morning, that an engine driver, who worked for LMS Railway returning home after his shift, noticed a glow within the theatre. As he approached the building, he realised that it was on fire. Shortly afterwards there was a tremendous roar and the flames exploded through the roof sending debris everywhere. One of the worst fires in the history of the town was raging. Prompt action to cal the Fire Brigade was too late to save the theatre and it was completely engulfed.

The fire had started about 2.30am in the centre of the front Stalls and caused almost certainly by a carelessly discarded cigarette butt. At time the heat was so intense it cracked the windows of the houses opposite and some of the residents' walls were so hot that fire hoses had to be played on them to prevent further conflagration. By daylight, the old, much loved theatre had all but gone. What remained standing were two chimneys and the wall that fronted Russell Street. It was this wall that almost certainly saved the rows of houses in the street and possibly the adjoining streets. At 9.30am the Fire Officer decided that the remains of the building were unsafe, and ordered their demolition. All that remained was a vast smouldering heap of twisted metal and blackened rubble – a sad memorial to The '*Col*'.

There were two brighter notes however. Peter, the theatre cat, had escaped from the blaze, and the film programme survived. The pictures for the three day booking were *Three Wise Guys*, *The Singing Vagabond* and the *British Paramount News*, some 12,000 feet of film in all. Whilst the projection room was wrecked, the fire had not broken into it, no doubt because of the efficiency of the Fire Brigade. Thankfully this did not happen, as had it have done so, the 12,000 feet of film would have caused a massive explosion.

Although the reproduction is not very clear, these two press photographs give an indication of the damage in The Coliseum *fire of 1936* (Evening Telegraph)

My recollections of The *New Coliseum* are few. I must have visited the place at some time during my boyhood, for I can dimly remember the long corridor at the rear entrance of the building. I am sure though, that we queued in that corridor and entered the auditorium from another way. Perhaps not, but I do remember snippets of the night of the fire.

At that time, I lived in Lime Street and my bedroom was at the rear of the house. I can recall standing at my parents' bedroom window in the front of the house and looking at the big red glow in the sky, and what seemed like giant sparks rising in the night air. My father told me in latter years that my mother was woken by a frightening noise and waking him, they both looked out and saw the glow from the fire. Sensing it was something out of the ordinary, they woke me so that I should see it.

My father, inquisitive as ever, quickly dressed and charged off on his bicycle, in company with a neighbour, towards the direction of the glow, of which he was certain was of a fire. He thought, as a shoe worker, that it was the shoe factory in Saint Peter's Avenue, but on arriving on the higher level of Saint Mary's Road, he was able to see flames, not from the factory as he expected, but from The *Coliseum*. He was stopped from getting any nearer. Later that day, along with my pals, I was able to get into Russell Street and I can recall the massive heap of rubble that had been the theatre, the smell that hung about in the air and the sight of the cracked windows in the houses opposite. That scene is a hazy recollection now, but I do remember the hushed atmosphere blanketing the street.

The loss of The '*Col*' had a profound effect upon the theatregoers of Kettering, and its loss in that way was beyond the belief of many. The realisation that an old friend had gone took time to register, and that the theatre, only recently refurbished with its up-to-date stage lighting not even used, was no more.

A new cinema/theatre was to rise 'phoenix fashion' on the site, and herald a new era of entertainment, but in the minds and hearts of many, it would never be the same.

This new super cinema was opened on Saturday 21 May 1938, and was called The *Savoy*, being the third super cinema which had been opened in Kettering within two years. Rising from the ashes of the former *New Coliseum*, The *Savoy* was a fitting tribute to the site which had seen entertainment of all kinds for 35 years.

It has to be admitted that the determination of its Managing Director, Jack Sherwood, and others, to re-build was exemplary, and provided the town with a continuance of fine entertainment for many more years. It still stands today, thought its future is threatened and the only site after 1974 still showing pictures in Kettering.

The *Savoy* was designed by C. Edmund Wilford of Leicester and built by Leighton (Contractors) of London, who were responsible for building cinemas up and down the country, and in particular, the *Odeons* for Deutsch. From the start as much local business was employed in its construction. Sand for the plasterwork was supplied by the Kettering Sand and Gravel Company; the sanitary engineering was by A. G. Miller; timber was supplied by Luck and Andrew; and decorative materials by the Montagu Wallpaper and Paint Company; Uniforms were supplied by the Kettering Industrial Co-operative Society.

The design was quite different from the original building. Because of the lay of the site it was still necessary to run the length parallel to Russell Street, but there the similarity ended. The building towered above the street and factories, dwarfing the modest houses that surrounded it.

Entrance was now directly off Russell Street through two sets of double doors which led to a foyer. To the right was the pay-desk and other services. To the left were the two sets of entrance doors to the Stalls. Art the far end of the foyer, stairs led to the Circle Lounge. On the right of the Lounge, double doors led to the centre of the Circle by a short flight of stairs. Services, which included the Manager's office and access to the projection room, were situated in the Circle Lounge.

Only when seated was it possible to appreciate the excellence of the interior décor. Tasteful colours led the eye to the huge Grecian Garden murals each side of the proscenium, the 'clouds' of which extended to the frieze running the length of the auditorium ceiling. The proscenium opening was 42 feet wide and arched away to the auditorium murals each side and into the décor of the ceiling plasterwork above. The proscenium was decorated with three artistic grilles, one each side and one above, which were adorned with artwork depicting musical notes. The whole interior was modelled in relief plaster mouldings and decorated in soft tones and hues.

The seating capacity was 774 in the Stalls and 357 in the Circle and was fitted out entirely with mottled plush in such a way that no matter where you sat, you had a good view of the stage. Furnishings and fittings were installed by Gaumont British Furnishings Limited.

The stage was 48 feet wide and 24 feet deep. There were seven dressing rooms, and a separate one for the orchestra. Usual stage fittings including trap doors, were included and there was a spacious orchestra pit.

The exterior of the building was in brick. All the 'services' were on the Russell Street side, which included, in addition to the new entrance, exit ways, the stage door and scenery dock entrance. The few windows on the façade were concealed effectively with decorative cast iron grilles.

The canopy over the entrance had a letterbox and an array of neon lighting. Above the canopy, a large 'fin' stretched up the building with the name SAVOY picked out in neon. Neon lighting also ran along the top of the building. The effect of the neon lights speeding across the building and down the fin was spectacular, lighting up the street so much that the residents close by could use the display to light their front rooms.

The *Savoy* ranked as one of the three modern cinemas in the town and it was to live up to the standard that its General Manager had pledged. The opening of the cinema/theatre was an event of the year. A special souvenir programme was presented to each dignitary and guest that night. In the programme, Harold Jackson spoke of his pleasure and feelings of succeeding to the management of so splendid a cinema-theatre as The *Savoy*. He also referred to his seven years as Manager of The *Coliseum* and pledged to represent the Savoy by giving its patrons the finest programmes available and to maintain a very high standard of efficiency. Seat prices at the time were Stalls 6d, 9d and 1s; Circle 1s 3d. Matinee prices were Stalls 4d and 6d, and the Circle 6d.

The front cover of the souvenir brochure

The opening ceremony started with the customary speeches by notable dignitaries followed by the Chairman of the Kettering

Mr. JACK SHERWOOD,
Managing Director of the new Savoy Cinema Luxury Theatre.

General Information.

Hours of Opening.

EVENING - 5-45 p.m.
MATINEES. Monday, Thursday, Saturday, at 2-30.
Doors open 2 p.m.

Prices of Admission (including Tax.)

EVENING.

Front Stalls	6d.
Centre ..	9d
Back ..	1/-
Balcony	1/3

MATINEES PRICES.
Stalls 4d. & 6d. Balcony 6d.

"Ardente" Hearing Equipment.

For the benefit of those Patrons with defective hearing the "Ardente" deaf aid equipment has been installed in this Theatre.

Earphones will be supplied Free of Charge on application to the Manager.

Messages.

Doctors or Professional expecting messages should leave their Names at the Pay Office and also with the Attendant, before taking their seats.

Telephone 2794.

★ 

Mrs. JACK SHERWOOD,
whose father the late Mr. Frank Payne built the original Coliseum in Russell Street.

Mr. HAROLD JACKSON,
Manager and Stage Director
of the Savoy Cinema Theatre.

May 21st, 1938.

Ladies and Gentlemen,

It is with pleasure I express in this letter my feelings in succeeding to the management of so splendid a Cinema-Theatre as the Savoy. Despite the welcome extended to me during my seven years as Manager of the Coliseum, I am very conscious of the great numbers whose acquaintance I have made and been able to serve.

I give you my assurance that in representing the Savoy I shall at all times endeavour to give you the finest programmes available, shown in comfortable and pleasant surroundings. Always at your service to investigate any complaints in the service of this Theatre.

My ambition is to maintain a very high standard of efficiency of staff, and my experience during twenty years, both in Management and Stage Direction, will always be foremost in giving you satisfaction. I sincerely trust that the very pleasant acquaintance of the past will be retained in the future.

Yours very faithfully,
HAROLD JACKSON,
Manager.

The inside of the souvenir brochure

Council performing the official opening. Amid fanfares and music, the first film programme began with a *Pathetone Weekly* (a magazine reel with musical interlude) followed with a Popeye cartoon and finally the feature film *Big City.*

Outside, before the opening ceremony, Russell Street was a bustling scene with crowds of people waiting to enter, or just milling around soaking up the atmosphere. Bathed in the changing colours from the cinema's neon, the scene was not unlike a Hollywood premiere right there in the heart of Kettering. So crowded was the street that those arriving by car were unable to reach the doors of the cinema without leaving their vehicles some distance away.

Jackson was to live up to his pledge for the following week there appeared on stage 'Troise and his Mandoliers', a top recording band of the decade. Other 'straight from a London season' shows were to follow, including the spectacular *Belle of New York.* Popular films of the day were regularly screened and top line stage and radio acts were presented. During the Second World War some very famous names were to appear on the Savoy stage. Reginald Foorte appeared on Monday 8 January 1940 bringing with him his

The Savoy *opening night, 1937*
(Evening Telegraph)

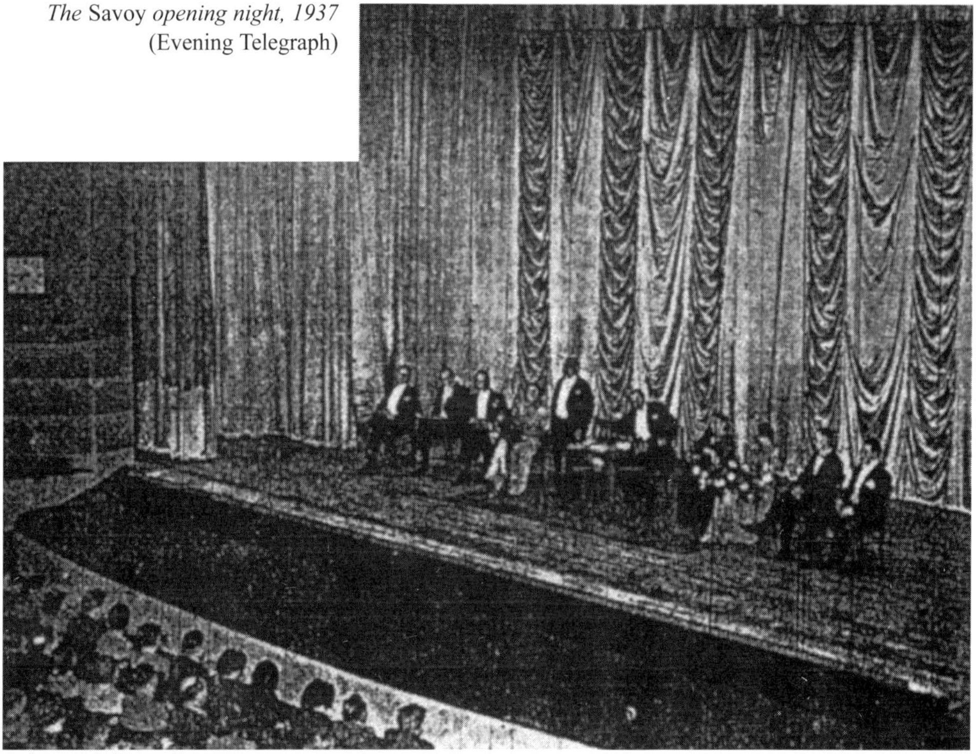

Moller Theatre Organ which later was to become the BBC theatre organ after the Corporation organ was destroyed by enemy action. Another organist had performed at The *Savoy*. It was Harold Ramsey, the famous electronic organist bringing with him an instrument few Kettering people had ever seen the likes of.

Interior – Savoy *Theatre*

There were many others too. Arthur Askey, Harry Hemsley (child impersonator), the 'Great Levante' (illusionist), Tommy Trinder, Sandy Powell, Will Fyffe, George Robey, Ella Shields (performing her famous song *Burlington Bertie*), Dickie Murdoch and the *Happidrome* radio show cast, the *ITMA* radio show cast, and so many more. Circuses also visited. 'Lord' John Sanger arrived for a week's booking bringing with him three very large elephants who were 'stabled' at the Angel Hotel off Dalkieth Place. Their walk, or should it be amble, back and forth through the streets for the two performances each day brought excitement to the children and adults alike and provided some of the best rhubarb sets on the town's allotments that year. They had arrived in town on a circus train.

Once, during the Second World War, the cinema was closed to the public, allowing the Princess Patricia's Canadian Light Infantry to be billeted until a local camp was prepared (thought to be Wicksteed Park).

When presenting pictures the cinema would open Monday to Saturday at 5.45pm and run a continuous performance, the main feature twice, and the support feature once. The news, trailers and any cartons were run twice. Matinees were Monday, Thursday and Saturday at 2.30pm, and then continuously right through to the end of the evening. Stage presentations were as advertised but were mostly either once nightly at 7.30pm or twice at 6pm and 8.30pm. Matinees were Thursday and Saturday at 2.30pm.

One special attraction which was to find a 'home' in The *Savoy* was, of course, the shows of the Kettering Operatic Society. For many years it was able to stage its superb productions in a fine theatre setting, and full advantage was taken. Later the Kettering Theatrical Society also performed on the stage. These shows are still remembered today. They were excellent, and without doubt enhanced by the venue in which they were played and the professional direction of Gladys Riseley.

In 1937, Jack Sherwood also took control of The *Empire* and he ran both cinemas until 1944 when Clifton Cinemas Limited brought The *Savoy* for £55,000. The sale did not however include The *Empire*, which Sherwood continued to run until 1947. Clifton Cinemas took over The *Savoy* on Friday 25 August 1944.

During the next few years The *Savoy* was to continue quality stage and screen presentations, including the well-remembered Sunday concerts, bringing to the town the top popular dance bands of the era. Ted Heath, Vic Lewis, Cyril Stapleton, the BBC Show Band, and others, were to delight the young (and not so young).

From 1948 until 1951 the winter seasons were taken over by the Northampton Repertory Company who, now billing the theatre under its name, presented weekly plays. Plays had limited popularity with Kettering audiences, but good houses were reasonably maintained. One play which appears to have been well received was *The Murder in the Red Barn*. The last play performed by the Company was *The Winslow Boy* on Saturday 21 October 1951.

The following day there was a Sunday concert, featuring Billy Ternant and his Orchestra. The theatre then closed for a while. In late November, it was announced that The *Savoy* would re-open under its own name on Christmas Eve 1951 with the pantomime *Red Riding Hood*, and booking would start immediately.

The pantomime played the theatre for two weeks followed at once by a second, *Cinderella*. To complete the holiday period entertainment, Roberts Brothers Circus was booked for a week. From that point it seems, the theatre was back in business.

An advert using the easily recognizable Savoy *logo which would become very familiar* (Evening Telegraph)

The cinema was later managed by Maurice Lee and the pattern of presentation was three months variety in the autumn and winter, with at least one pantomime at, or after, Christmas. The remaining months were devoted to film performances, and prices were 1s for Front Stalls, and 1s 3d for Rear Stalls, Rear Circle 2s and Front Circle 2s 9d. For stage shows the prices would average 2s 6d, 3s 6d and 4s 6d (reserved) and 1s 6d (unreserved).

Personal recollections of The *Savoy* revolve mainly around stage productions, particularly during the Second World War. I liked The *Savoy*. It was a fine modern theatre and equal to many London houses which, of course, were too expensive to visit often. I remember the visit of Reginald Foorte with his Moller Theatre Organ and the sight of the 'works' of this massive instrument as the curtains were drawn back during each performance to reveal the might of the organ assembled on the stage – and taking up most of it. Then there was the time when, as a pupil of the old Central School, I was taken to hear a performance by the wartime London Philharmonic Orchestra which wakened my liking for popular classical music.

A few years on, and it was the band shows which visited the theatre often. I can still remember the fabulous concert by Ted Heath and his Music which, by over running, held up the evening screen performance. Perhaps the best memories of all as a cinema were the 1950s 'Sci-fi' films. I reckon The *Savoy* showed them all, and on a big screen too.

I was to have the privilege of working on that vast stage with the Kettering Theatrical Society. One show stands out as a classic memory. One evening, during a week's run by the Society of the musical *Kismet*, the 'stays' that held steady the 18 feet high scenery, came adrift, and alongside other members of the stage-crew, I had to hold it upright throughout the 30 minutes or so whilst the scene was played out on the stage. The wavering of the scenery must have amused many in the audience that night.

Star Cinemas of Leeds acquired the theatre in 1967. By that time Bingo had been introduced alongside the film and stage performances and remained a bedfellow until Sunday 25 February 1968 when for the usual matinee performance, *Bonnie and Clyde* became the last film to be shown in the original *Savoy*. That evening, Bingo was played as usual and at 10pm The *Savoy* shut its doors bringing an era to a close.

The theatre underwent extensive alterations converting the former Stalls into a Bingo hall and transforming an extended Circle into a first floor luxury cinema with seating for 465 with complimentary ultra-modern furnishings and décor.

The Savoy *projection equipment during the 1960s* (Evening Telegraph)

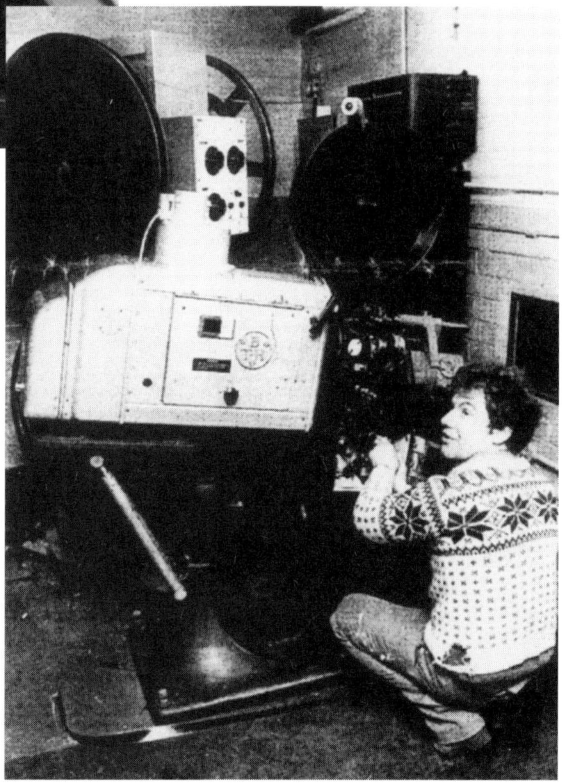

...and not forgetting the projectionist, who was soon destined to take over completely (Evening Telegraph)

The official opening was on Monday 9 September 1967 by the Mayor of Kettering, Alderman R. L. Denny, starting with a full civic reception in the Royal Hotel followed by a ceremony at The Savoy. The film chosen for the opening was *The Charge of the Light Brigade*, starring Trevor Howard, John Gielgud and Vanessa Redgrave, who all sent tributes. At the reception relics of the famous 'Charge' by the 'gallant 600' were displayed, which included an original Lancer's helmet, as well as the preserved head of 'Roland' the horse ridden in the 'Charge' by the Earl of Cardigan.

From the reception the guests were escorted to The *Savoy* by four horsemen dressed as Lancers. Vehicles from the 108th Recovery Regiment (TA) escorted the mayoral car. Crowds waiting in Russell Street saw the parade, which was reminiscent of the opening 30 years earlier. Inside the cinema, another 200 guests were joined by the VIPs, where the Mayor, heralded by a fanfare of trumpets, declared the new cinema open.

Many people were turned away that night as the cinema quickly filled and the first performance in the new *Savoy* began. As for the ground floor, it too received refurbishment, and continued as a Bingo hall.

After Star Cinemas had taken over in 1967, mixing cinema with Bingo
(Evening Telegraph)

The *Savoy* continued in this way until Saturday 7 September 1973, when it was closed once more for yet further conversion, this time into twin 'studio' cinemas. The last film to show was *Lady Caroline Lamb* starring Sarah Miles and Jon Finch.

In the early 1970s it was the trend to carve up large auditoria in large cinemas to create mini-cinemas with postage stamp screens, and such a development befell The *Savoy* under the Star Cinemas banner, though fortunately the screens were a respectable size in relation to the auditorium.

The *Studios 1 and 2* cinemas were created within the first floor of the old *Savoy* theatre. The Bingo hall was retained on the ground floor and there were separate entrances through the foyer into each one. By this time, The *Granada* was the only other cinema open in Kettering.

The conversion was accomplished within twelve days and consisted of a dividing wall lengthways through the existing auditorium giving an almost equal dimension to the two cinemas. The wall was supposedly fully sound insulated, but one could detect a slight seepage of sound, one to the other, particularly during very loud passages on soundtracks.

Contrasting colour schemes were introduced, and wall-to-wall carpeting gave a bright and modern look to the studio style cinemas. Both were fitted with psychedelic lighting effects which were used between film programmes. The projection room remained unaltered and served two screens with single system projection systems.

From the Evening Telegraph *of Easter 1973*

The 'twins' opened on Friday 20 April 1973 with *Studio 1* showing *The Ten Commandments* (1956) starring Charlton Heston and Yul Brynner. *Studio 2* opened with *Cabaret* (1972) with Lisa Minelli and Michael York. The whole complex comprising of the cinemas and Bingo took on the title of the Kettering Entertainment Centre.

The interior of Studio 1 (Kettering Museum)

The screen and proscenium of Studio 1 (Kettering Museum)

EMI acquired the Centre a few years later and subsequently closed the Bingo operation. The Star Group of Companies however, held the lease for the cinemas and continued to operate The *Studio* cinemas. Hamblin Leisure, a county based company, took over the whole building and re-opened the Bingo operation. Star Cinemas continued the lease with the new company, and the cinemas remained open.

The opening week (Evening Telegraph)

On Thursday 24 January 1985, the twin cinemas closed yet again. According to the Star Group, the cinemas had been losing money for some time. The Manageress, Margaret Osborne, and Allan Gray, the projectionist, along with eight other staff lost their jobs. The Bingo club continued to operate.

The last films to show were *Gremlins* (1984) along with an 'olde tyme' show which featured two silent shorts one of which was *Barefoot Boy* (1910) and included in the show was an organ interlude performed by 68 year old George Tingle.

An amusing anecdote to this last performance was that as *Barefoot Boy* was being projected, it started to rip apart in the projector, but skilful work by the assembled team projectionists saved the show as they hand-cranked the film through the projector whilst another staff member flicked a ruler across the lens to give the screened picture an 'old style' flicker.

Over 200 people were turned away on the last night. In a poignant speech Alan Gray said 'If you lot had turned up in the past, we wouldn't have been closing down now'.

With The *Granada* now long turned over to Bingo, and The *Studios* closed, Kettering now had no cinema or motion picture performances since 'living pictures' had started 88 years previously.

The Kettering Entertainment Centre (Kettering Museum)

But films *did* return to the old theatre site. In Easter 1986, Mr Ashley Whyatt, leased the two cinemas and undertook a programme of refurbishment. At first, only *Studio 1* was brought back into use, and it opened on Easter Monday with a matinee performance of *Return to Oz*, a Disney production which left much to be desired in the up-dated treatment of a children's classic. A goodly number of patrons had to be turned away from the matinee because all 140 seats were occupied. *Studio 2* refurbishment finished shortly afterwards and re-opened as unceremoniously as *Studio 1*.

Ashley Whyatt was known locally for his cinema operations, for he also ran the *Forum Suite* at Corby and the newly activated *Bentley* at Burton Latimer, formerly known as The *Electric Palace*. The Kettering *Studios* received a new name. Taking the name of Kettering's twinned town in America, the Kettering and Burton Latimer cinemas each became known as The *Ohio*.

When work was fully completed to both auditoria, the heating had been improved, some new seating installed, and new lighting for the foyer. The projection system had also been improved.

The success hoped for was only to last a short time, and by the end of the decade, both cinemas had become less popular, as many patrons, mostly the young, preferred to travel to the multiplex at Milton Keynes than frequent the progressively shabbier Kettering screen, and closure was on the cards once more.

In 1990, Brian McFarlane took over The *Ohios*, and he began a programme of further refurbishment, equipping the two cinemas with up-dated projection equipment and sound systems. Retaining the *Ohio* banner, he began with screen 2 re-seating it at 160, and to a high standard, presenting a cosy and comfortable auditorium with an acceptable sized screen. The sound system was up-graded to full Dolby surround, and he changed its name and status to *Ohio 1*.

The remaining screen (originally screen 1) also received new seating which numbered 140. The projection system was replaced and Dolby Stereophonic sound was installed. Both screens were programmed to run two shows nightly, with extra matinee shows during school holidays. A whole range of films to cater for all tastes was screened utilising the twin cinemas at different times of the day and evening. This worked well until 1996, when again the situation was serious.

Brian confessed to me that he did not know just how much longer he could continue. On the evening I visited, two weeks before Christmas, there were just two patrons in *Ohio 1*. In a population of over 50,000, only two people had bothered to go and see a cracking film. The other screen had not opened.

His dilemma was beyond his ability to escape. Because of low returns he could not book the latest releases and he had only a few supporters backing his efforts. There would be some respite over the holiday period, but what then?

Eight months later, The *Ohios* had gone. It was the story of The *Empire* and *Granada* all over again.

SAVOY Tel.: KETTERING 2794

SAVOY TEL. 2794

SAVOY

SAVOY Tel.: KETTERING 2794

Doors open Today 6.15, Thursday, Saturday 2 p.m.

JULIE ANDREWS

HAWAII A

Today 7.30; Thurs., Sat. 3.15, 7.30

FLOATING FORTRESS U

Today 6.35; Thurs., Sat. 2.20, 6.35

Owing to the length of the film, there will be an intermission for Coffee and Ice-Cream

BINGO: SUNDAY AFTERNOON, WEDNESDAY & FRIDAY EVENINGS

Join the Biggest and Best Bingo Club in the Midlands

Movies showing from Friday August 30th (7 days)

OHIO CINEMA KETTERING

☎ Kett 515130

NAKED GUN 2½ (12) 7.30pm & 9.30pm

SILENCE OF THE LAMBS (18) 7.30pm

EDWARD SCISSORHANDS (PG) 9.30pm Also Sat 3pm & Sun 4pm

TEENAGE MUTANT NINJA TURTLES II (PG) Sat 3pm & Sun 4pm

OHIO CINEMAS

RUSSELL STREET, KETTERING ☎ 515130

MOVIES SHOWING FROM FRIDAY 14th FEBRUARY

THE ADDAMS FAMILY (PG)

Fri 5pm & 9.15pm. Sat 3pm, 5pm & 9.15pm

Sun 4pm & 9.15pm. Mon-Thurs 3pm, 5pm & 9.15pm

FREDDIES DEAD

The Final Nightmare (18) 7.30pm & 9.15pm

BILL & TEDS BOGUS JOURNEY (PG) 7.30pm

AN AMERICAN TAIL 2 (U)

Sat 3pm, Sun 4pm, Mon-Thurs 3pm

ALL SEATS £1.70

FEB '92

OHIO CINEMAS

RUSSELL STREET, KETTERING

TELEPHONE 0536 515130

MOVIES SHOWING FROM FRIDAY 19th MARCH TO THURSDAY 25th MARCH

UNDER SIEGE (15) with STEVEN SEAGAL 7.30pm Nightly

RESERVOIR DOGS (18) 9.20pm nightly

THE BODYGUARD (15) with KEVIN COSTNER and WHITNEY HOUSTON 9pm Nightly

HELLRAISER III (18) 7.30pm Nightly

HOME ALONE 2 (PG) Matinees only Saturday 3pm, Sunday 3.30pm

HONEY, I BLEW UP THE KID (U) Matinees only Saturday 3pm, Sunday 3.30pm

AFTERNOONS £1.80 AND EVENINGS £2.00

SAVOY Tel. KETTERING 2794

TODAY: Tony Curtis, Jerry Lewis — BOEING, BOEING A

THE BIG, BIG SCOOP OF THE YEAR

BREAKING ALL RECORDS EVERYWHERE

Sunday: Doors open 5.45, Mon., Thurs., & Sat. 1.15; Tues. 5.0

Sunday 8.5, Mon., Thurs. & Sat. 1.35, 5.10, 8.50; Tues. 5.10, 8.50

Lex Barker — VICTIM 5 A

Sunday 6.20, Mon., Thurs. & Sat. 3.25, 7.5, Tuesday 7.5

POPPIES' NIGHT TUESDAY NIGHT — COME AND MEET THE PLAYERS

RESERVOIR DOGS with Harvey Keitel, Tim Roth, Michael Madsen and Chris Penn. A violent and provocative thriller. (cert 18) 7.15pm nightly

HELL RAISER III (Hell on Earth) Starring Doug Bradley as 'Pinhead' with Terry Farrell and Paula Marshall (cert 18) 9.30pm nightly

BRAM STOKER'S Dracula (18) Love Never Dies with Gary Oldman & Anthony Hopkins (cert 18) 9pm nightly

A FEW GOOD MEN with Jack Nicholson, Demi Moore & Tom Cruise (cert 15) 7.15pm nightly

HONEY I BLEW UP THE KID (cert U) 6.30pm nightly plus matinee Sat 3pm, Sun 3.30pm

Macaulay C... HOME AL... LOST IN N... (cert PG) mat... Sat 3pm, Su...

Walt Dis... BEAU... THE B... (cert U) mati... Sat 1pm, S...

What of the remainder of the old *Savoy* building? The Bingo club remained, but the original décor had long gone. The precious, wonderful stage was moribund, and the seats given over to people who sat pinning hopes of wealth on the luck of a set of numbers, with little knowledge or care for the hallowed place they occupied, or the ghosts of the past great stars still lurking within the walls. And soon afterwards, even this Bingo club was forced to close.

Today, the building stands empty and unused. It will probably be demolished, and if the lessons of the losses of the old *Odeon* and Central Hall have not been learned, then Kettering will have lost another part of its cultural heritage.

The cinema's dark. Hidden from view, the graciously adorned interior is now decayed and peeling. The once pleasant foyer, its atmosphere of excitement and anticipation for what was to come, now just an empty space, its walls austere and un-inviting, scrawled with obscene graffiti from the yobbish vandals who continually burgle and plunder.

In this building, over 60 years of entertainment of all kinds have taken place. Then, the town's people loved it, and those living by it respected its presence. Kettering must stop shrugging its collective shoulders, and do something about it soon, or yet another piece of cultural history will be lost forever.

Projection and technical information

Coliseum:

The projection box was situated at the Rear Stalls and was asbestos lined. There was a single Pathe Imperial mute projector. Later, a second projector was installed to allow longer films to be shown, but the make and date are obscure, although it was likely to have been a second Imperial. The projectors were motorised and used carbon arc lamps of an unknown make. There was also a slide lantern

New Coliseum:

The old projection box at the rear of the Stalls was removed and a new one built behind the rear Balcony wall. Two Kalee 7 projectors were installed, with British Talking Picture (BTP) sound heads (sound-on-film). The amplification system was by BTP.

The screen was on the rear wall of the stage and speaker horns were mounted to emit sound through grilles around the proscenium. The light source was by Kalee arc lamps. A slide lantern was installed. Three-colour stage lighting was installed supplying overhead battens and footlights. It was controlled by a switchboard and dimmers from side stage (actors' left). It was never used before being destroyed in the great fire.

Savoy:

The Savoy was well equipped for both pictures and stage. The projection equipment installed when the Savoy was built is obscure, but most likely to be two Kalee 7 models. The arc lamps were Kalee. The sound heads were BTP and it is known hat the sound system was by British Acoustic. The projection room layout was from left to right looking towards the front wall was, Slide Projector/Follow Spot number2/Projector 2/Controls for Screen tabs and sound/Projector 1/ Follow Spot number 1. The amplifier racks were on the back wall of the room. Non-sync right side wall.

The stage was 48 feet wide and 24 feet deep. The stage lighting board was situated across left and the 'fly' position was to the actors' right. The stage lighting was three colours and there were stage spots situated in the 'house'. For stage shows, the two Follow Spots in the projection room were used for the artistes.

The screen was 'flown' for stage shows. When the large Cinemascope screen was installed it was also able to be moved for stage shows and had variable side masking. The projection equipment changed at an obscure time, likely when Cinemascope and Wide Screen were installed in the 1950s. The sound system also changed to RCA, at least that is what I remember from my occasional visits. More modern Kalee projectors and Peerless Arcs were installed and Kalee Varamorph anamorphic lenses fitted. The Savoy was fitted out with an 'Ardente' Hearing system to assist patrons with hearing difficulties, and in the early days, a paging system for doctors and other professionals visiting the cinema.

Studios 1 and 2:

Two Ross GC3 projectors (one for each screen, fitted with RCA sound heads and with RCA amplification equipment. A Westrex long-running tower system. BTH 2,000 watt Xenon light source and anamorphic lenses for each projector. The projection room is 50 feet long, which incorporates accommodation for both screens. There are no details of improvements to the sound system to present the film sound technology of the day, but it is unlikely that Dolby would have been installed in the Studio days. Though records cannot confirm, it is certain that a Kalee 21 replaced one of the Ross projectors prior to 1989.

Ohio:

Screen 1 (ex Screen 2) Kalee 21 projector with RCA sound head and RCA amplification. Tower system. Later, a Dolby Stereophonic sound system was installed. Xenon light source

Screen 2 (ex Screen1) Until 1989 – a Ross GC3 projector with RCA sound head and amplification. From 1989 – a Kalee 21 projector with RCA sound head system. From 1995 – a Monee projector with RCA sound system with Stereophonic sound. Xenon light source.

THE KETTERING ELECTRIC PAVILION

THE GAUMONT PAVILION

THE GAUMONT

The *Kettering Electric Pavilion*, to give it its full name, or '*Pav*' as it was fondly called, was Kettering's first purpose-built cinema; the first to run continuous performances; the first to show 'talkies' and one of the first to be fitted with a new 'wide screen. It was foremost in the screening of British films, most of them reaching its screens at one time or another.

The '*Pav*' changed very little in its lifetime structurally and architecturally. The frontage remained right up until 1953, and today, had it survived in its original style, would surely have been a listed building. Sadly, like many of its kind, it has gone – now but a memory.

About 1912, the only venues in Kettering for motion pictures were *Vint's Palace*, the *Avenue* and the Victoria Hall. Variety, plays and other stage presentations were their business, and the 'living pictures' were fill-ins. As is known, travelling Bioscopes brought with them whole evenings of pictures but the venues themselves were not given over to motion pictures completely. Not one had even a projection room and little more than a roll up screen.

Cinema had advanced beyond the single reeler. Two and even three reelers were becoming fashionable and more importantly, they had 'stars'. Cinema was able to provide complete entertainment in its own right. Buildings dedicated to the presentation of motion pictures were being built or converted all over the country, and the Cinema had arrived. Dedicated to the purpose of showing films, they had proper projection rooms and static equipment, seating, and specially designed screens. Cinema had broken free from its shackles.

There was room for new enterprise in Kettering and surprisingly it came from outside the town. At the end of the High Street, close to Bakehouse Hill, and incidentally, only a few yards away from the Victoria Hall, the site of the residence owned by Mr John Newman came onto the market in 1912, and was bought by the Rotherham Electric Theatre Company. Construction started almost immediately on what was publicised at the time as 'a picture palace in keeping with the importance of the town.'

The Kettering Electric Pavilion *on a date unknown, but certainly in the cinema's early life* (D. Wharton)

The new purpose built cinema opened at 5.30pm on Saturday 10 May 1913, and was named *The Kettering Electric Pavilion*, a fine but unwieldy name which was soon to be shortened to The *Electric Pavilion*, and by most, to The '*Pav*'. The first screening was at 6pm, and was continuous until 10.45pm. The programme was *When Lee Surrendered, Interrupted Honeymoon, On Account of a Transfer* and *Fog*.

Prices were Front seats 2d, Centre 4d and 6d, Rear seats 9d. The cinema was immediately popular. Patrons liked the newfound freedom of being able to 'walk up' at any time they wished.

> The report of the opening spoke of
> 'this new brightly lit palace for the pictures [which] is a welcome addition to Kettering's wealth of entertainment. The pictures are clear and well exhibited in a building specially designed for them. It is comfortable and airy and one can walk up virtually any time and is usually assured a seat. Its very name swells the breast with pride, and so it should.'

The *Pavilion* could seat 650 in a single auditorium with no Balcony. In the original plans, a Balcony was to be constructed later. Why this was so is not clear, perhaps the money ran out with the construction of the distinctive exterior, or another of the company's projects elsewhere took priority, who knows? But the plans were never brought to fruition due in the end to the intervention of the Great War the following year. A raked floor was provided however, and patrons could see the screen comfortably – that is if you did not sit in the front rows.

Whilst the interior was comfortable, it did not however live up to the rather more classic architecture of the exterior. It was a fairly simple design reminiscent of the Victorian era. Entrance was by six marble steps leading into the vestibule and up to the central pay desk. Either side of the entrance were two tall circular pillars supporting the upper masonry. Each side of the entrance, shop fronts had been built, to the left when facing the cinema were the office, storage space and circular stairs to the projection room. On the opposite side was a shop occupied by a hairdresser and milliner. Later, this became part of the cinema.

On the upper facia there were three ornate panels, each separated by a small window. On these panels were inscribed the words KETTERING, ELECTRIC and PAVILION. Above was a gothic style arch. Below its parapet was a semi-circular drop window which, it is thought, was the projection room window. On the roof of the cinema there was a small tower which was part of the ventilation system and from this rose a mast which carried a decorative globe which was lit up at night.

On the front of the building hung four very large electric globes lights and the stonework was illuminated by 48 electric lamps. It is no wonder that it was called The *Electric Pavilion* for its lights bathed the High Street and the whole of Bakehouse Hill.

Entrance to the auditorium was by two sets of very large and heavy doors each side of the pay-desk. Once inside, big heavy curtains were encountered, which acted as a light trap. Later, another set of heavy doors, were fitted in place of the curtains and this created a cave-like space between the two sets of doors. I remember as a boy tugging open the doors as they closed behind me and being engulfed in what seemed to me total blackness whilst negotiating the second door. It was made worse by coming in out of the daylight. It was a little scary.

The interior was described at the time as being 'comfortable but modest' – and that it was. The walls of the auditorium were plainly decorated. Every few feet buttresses rose from floor to the roof which served as both supports for the girder work and as ventilation shafts. At the top of the walls ran a plasterwork frieze and false parapet. There was no false ceiling and the girders supporting the roof were visible.

The proscenium was modelled on the style of a Roman Pavilion with an arch and fluted columns, which were stone-effect and gilt. Plasterwork scrolls and ornamental carvings filled the arch, with cherub adornments.

The cinema had no stage to talk of, only a few feet deep, but it was quite high with a patterned canvas front. In sound picture days the non-sync equipment was under the stage and the canvas illuminated. The tabs may have been opened from there also. The screen was on the back wall, as the stage was only a few feet deep. To the right side of the stage was an exit directly in to Wadcroft.

There was no cross gangway at the rear of the Stalls, as the seats ran right up to the rear wall. The toilet facilities were off to the right hand side of the auditorium, and anyone sitting left of centre or in the left side block of seats was required to walk down to the front, along by the stage, and half way up the right aisle to reach the entrances to the toilets.

The *Pavilion* was quite steeply raked. If one was to walk from the rear of the Stalls down towards the screen by the time the front was reached you were in a brisk sprint, only to slow dramatically in climbing the other aisle to reach the object of need. Likewise on the return, one would face a climb back to one's seat. The same problem arose with the sales assistant who always stood at the front Stalls, assuming she got there safely after having entered the cinema with her tray via High Street.

I digress, for those anecdotes were to apply in later years. For Kettering, the new purpose-built cinema was very welcome indeed. Its opening was a great occasion.

During the silent era, music for films was played mostly on the piano by Florence Martin who had a mirror to assist her because of the high level of the screen. However, for the prestigious pictures, accompaniment was augmented with a fine little orchestra although there was little room for more than a 'bijou' outfit. There were occasional 'musical interludes' by local musicians when important pictures were shown, but quite where they were situated is also a mystery as the front rows of the seats were quite near to the screen – the proverbial 'neck-breakers'.

The *Pav.* became the premier picture house until 1920 when The *Victoria Picture House* and The *Empire* came upon the scene. Its advertising was almost entirely by handbill and poster. Very few adverts appear in the local press until the 1920s. It vied with its two competitors and showed some of the most important films of the day and just about the whole repertoire of the Charlie Chaplin films.

The cinema became The Gaumont Pavilion *in 1929, this picture being taken soon afterwards. Regardless of its full name it was always known as the* 'Pav' (D. Wharton)

The cinema changed hands in 1919, with Messrs Hutton and Shapiro of Nottingham taking control, but there was little change to the building in their time. And in 1927 the ownership changed again, when the *Pav.* was bought out by Denham (Midland) Cinemas Limited, part of the Gaumont-British Picture Corporation, and its name changed to The *Gaumont Pavilion*.

In late November 1929, The *Pav.* closed for a short time to be 'wired for sound'. 'Talkies' had already found their way to Kettering with short, mainly musical or variety act films exhibited at The *Victoria Picture House*. Features like Jolson's *Jazz Singer* and *Singing Fool* (which, it is little known, were only part 'talkie') had already filled cinemas elsewhere that had been wired up and now the 'all talking' pictures were following fast as studios geared up too the new medium.

The debut of the 'talkies' at The *Pav.* was on Monday 9 December 1929 with *Perfect Alibi* (aka *Alibi*) (1929). The programme ran for six days and also included a sound cartoon *Osprey House* and the *Movietone News*. The debut was a huge success and a review in the *Evening Telegraph* the next day said:

> **'Successful talkie at the Kettering Pavilion**
>
> It was appropriate that the first voice on the screen to be heard was that of the late T. P. O'Connors at the Kettering Electric Pavilion where sound pictures made their debut last night. Few Kettering people have ever heard the well-known T. P. speak but those who did say they have never heard him more distinctly than the Kettering audience did. It was very easy to imagine the great statesman, whose death is recorded amongst the numerous items in the Movietone News, standing in the Hall quietly talking to the audience. Anyone who loves dramas without too much love interest and where the plot is compounded in a battle of wits rather than the endless competition of combats will find the ideal picture in "The Perfect Alibi", a full 100% talking picture which will be showing all the week. The plot is easy to follow as is the dialogue. Supporting is a highly amusing sound cartoon "Osprey House" and a silent comedy [not advertised] which relies on clever plot rather than ludicrous acting as entertainment. Altogether a good show, bearing in mind that nothing is perfect during its trial run, the clarity of the talkie is praiseworthy.'

Whilst I have tended to leave the technical detail until the end of the cinema chapters, it is important to make mention here of what is an interesting situation. 'Talkies' had been experimented with for many years, and two specific items were developed – sound-on-disc and sound-on-film. The disc system required a player, usually at the rear of the projector to which it was synchronised. The sound track was recorded on a sixteen-inch disc and the picture and sound were simultaneously played, resulting in a 'talkie' picture. Sound-on-film was the photographing of electrical sound impulses and transferring these optically to the film. Disc was inferior in quality to sound-on-film and liable to get out of synchronisation wit the pictures. Sound-on-film, of course, did not.

When Warner Brothers began the sound era in 1926, they used the sophisticated disc system developed by the Western Electric and Bell Telephone Company, called Vitaphone, and premiered it at their theatre on Broadway on Friday 6 August 1926 with Don Juan. William Fox had brought out system and rights to sound-on-film processes and had produced sound shorts by this system well before this. However, he chose to perfect his system and he did not introduce it to the public until Friday 21 January 1927. RCA Photophone had also developed sound-on-film. Films were made using both systems until 1930 when by international agreement, sound-on-film was declared the standard for sound pictures, and the disc system, almost extinct by then anyway, was declared dead.

Anyway, what has all this to do with The *Pav*? Well, we know that The *Victoria Picture House* had shown 'talkies', albeit only sound shorts, and they were probably sound-on-disc. The film *Perfect Alibi* which gave The *Pav.* its 'talkie' debut was written and directed by Roland West for United Artists. United Artists were part of a group of studios who had agreements with Western Electric's subsidiary ERPI who were marketing sound-on-film systems. On the same programme was *Movietone News*, a product of Fox which began life in 1929 using the sound-on-film system. The cartoon was disc system. The *Pavilion* was therefore wired for both systems. This would have been the normal installation for this period though the system was changed to sound-on-film within a year. Oddly however, the programme for the following week was all-silent, being *Eternal Love* (1929) starring John Barrymore. Records are obscure as to whether *Jazz Singer* was ever shown in Kettering.

The *Gaumont Pavilion* continued to be a major house in the town right into the 1950s. I remember seeing my favourite female star, Shirley Temple, at The *Pav.* in most of her films, especially *Captain January* (1936) with Guy Kilbee.

This story of a shipwrecked little girl was special for me as in one scene she walks towards a door, turns to the camera – and winks. For this seven year old, that wink was for me alone. Ah, the magic of cinema!

The *Pav.* continued bringing pictures to Kettering audiences right up to the 1950s, but by now it was showing its age. There had been little change to its appearance, internally or externally, and its owners, by this time the Rank Organisation, scheduled the old cinema for a total refurbishment. The *Pav.* closed on Wednesday 2 September 1953, with the last film to show being *Thunder Bay* (1953).

Forty years of pictures in this much loved cinema had momentarily come to an end. It had seen, and pioneered, the great change from silent to sound. Never again were we to see one of the projection staff creep through the sliding door left side of the small platform stage just before the end of the features and out again after the start. Was it he who entertained us with the strains of the selections from *White Horse Inn* and similar shows, or was he just opening the curtains? Maybe just giving Archie the slip? We may never know.

Within three weeks the old *Pavilion* was to undergo a transformation where Kettering picture goers were to see the old frontage lost beneath a modern façade for six years – and then lost for good.

The upper part of the old building was retained. The large panels bearing the words KETERING, GAUMONT and PAVILION were the first to go, being replaced with the word GAUMONT in the two outer panels, the centre one remaining blank. The shop fronts either side of the entrance were removed and replaced by attractive brickwork with entrances to the office on one side and to the services and projection room on the other. The old pillars either side of the entrance were encased within an attractive hardwood feature, and between them had been constructed a canopy with down-lights illuminating the entrance doors. The doors comprised two sets of double doors with modern glazing. Above were three large modern fanlights.

Entrance to the cinema was by the original six steps, but these had now been revamped in white mottled tile and black edge strips. The pay-box was still central with entrances each side. The new vestibule was tastefully decorated with down-lights and publicity areas. Once inside however, the changes were more dramatic.

The old *Pavilion* had no foyer. In the renovation this was changed and after passing through the foyer doors patrons could mingle in a small bright comfortable vestibule before entering the auditorium by two further sets of double doors. The small vestibule was furnished in such a way giving a luxury feel to the cinema and utilising the 'tunnel-like' entrances so reminiscent of the old *Pavilion*.

The auditorium had been competently refurbished. The obtrusive roof girders were completely concealed by a false ceiling dotted with down lighting in the form of spotlights. The ventilation shafts had been concealed within wall cladding. The interior was redecorated in soft shades, the toilets were completely rebuilt and modernised. New seating was installed and the seating capacity, reduced to accommodate the new foyer, was 550.

The most prominent feature of the old *Pavilion*, its proscenium, had been totally concealed behind the modern clean lines of a new one. The ornate plasterwork was removed, including the cherubs which were seemingly to be lost forever – what lovely museum pieces they would have been. The small stage was remodelled and a new wide screen installed in front of the original leaving virtually no stage at all. The proscenium was effectively lit giving a pleasant fusing of light. Deep carpet completed the luxury of the auditorium but the rake remained and was still evident, although to a lesser degree.

Altogether the appearance of the cinema was very pleasing indeed and I remember being impressed on my visits. New projection equipment was installed and the new wide screen was an admirable size for the auditorium giving a clean shape to the projected picture. It was brilliant with VistaVision and looked good in Cinemascope.

After refurbishment in 1953 as The Gaumont. (Evening Telegraph)

Kettering picture goers expressed their approval when on the re-opening night they thronged the High Street and Bakehouse Hill to witness the event. On Friday evening, 25 September 1953, just three weeks after the old *Pav*. closed, the cinema opened again as The *Gaumont*. What an occasion it was. One could be forgiven for thinking it was another Hollywood premier. Scenes reminiscent of The *Savoy* and *Regal* openings were enacted again. To open their new theatre, Rank had sent along one of their top stars, Joan Collins, dressed like the young movie queen she was. She was adored by the crowd, and the ceremony was reported in the following day's *Evening Telegraph*:

> 'The transformation of Kettering's oldest cinema into a luxurious palace of entertainment with the towns widest and brightest screen was warmly applauded last night by an enthusiastic audience. Within the period of twenty-one days Kettering residents had watched their oldest entertainment house having its face lifted. High stone steps and pokey pay-box, shop windows and old fashioned doors have been banished. Instead there stands a glittering new theatre on the structure of the old but streamlined, cleverly decorated and brilliantly lit.
>
> Joan Collins, 20 year old star of many British films arrived wearing a black sequinned cocktail dress and white fur stole and her deep tan was evident of her return from location in Spain where she has just finished her latest picture. Crowds lined the High Street on both sides filling the pavements. Such was the magnitude of people that Miss Collins was heard to ask "is it the cinema they have come to see?" The mayor of Kettering in his opening address said "this theatre has more than just luxury, it has tradition. We remember it as an old cinema when the slides were scratched with a pin and the Musical Director was a solitary pianists positioned beneath the screen. It speaks well for the entertainment at this house in that it has stood the test of time and is still with us today. Miss Collins then received a pair of golden scissors and cut the mauve tape draped across the wide screen and the first pictures in the remodelled cinema began.'

The opening programme was *Genevieve* (1953) starring the popular quartet of Kay Kendall, John Gregson, Dinah Sheridan and Kenneth More. The supporting feature was *Murder at 3am* (1947) starring Dennis Price. The current issue of *Gaumont British News* completed the performance. The tradition was truly to be continued, for after a nine day run, the programme to follow was *Innocents in Paris* (1953) starring Alastair Sim and Margaret Rutherford, all of them British films.

I can remember that opening night. I was working at The *Granada* at the time and Friday was my night off. I milled around the High Street soaking up the atmosphere. The *Gaumont* looked a picture, and I felt a warm respect for the re-birth of Kettering's oldest cinema.

The opening night of The Gaumont *Friday 25 September 1953* (Evening Telegraph)

During its short life, The *Gaumont* was to provide good entertainment for its patrons, plus having the occasional drama. It was very much a cousin to The *Odeon* sharing its newsreel and often its Manager. There was once a small fire, but it caused very little damage and did not even result in a closure. Sadly the tradition of good entertainment could not save The *Gaumont* and only after six years, it was to close.

Notice of closure was given on Saturday 3 October 1959. the last show was *Last Train from Gun Hill* (1959) starring Kirk Douglas, Anthony Quinn and Earl Holliman. It was described as a 'good suspense and action Western culminating in a 'High Noon' situation'. The old picture house went out fighting and its doors closed for the final time at 10.45pm on Saturday 10 October 1959. For one person, it was the end of an era. The chief projectionist 'Archie' Mason had shown pictures in the cinema most of his working life. Westerns were his favourite pictures, and what a fitting, though sad, finale for Archie.

Demolition of The Gaumont, *revealing the interior of the old* Pavilion. *The proscenium arch pillars can clearly be seen* (Evening Telegraph)

The people of Kettering did not really understand what was happening when The *Gaumont* closed, for it was just a year later when its cousin across the way, The *Odeon*, also closed. Effectively the Rank Organisation stopped showing pictures in Kettering. Because of the two cinemas closing so close to each other, Kettering cinema goers felt bitter towards the company and perhaps justifiably so. The *Gaumont* was a popular cinema and although audiences had dwindled, it was well used. Did the owners think that with closing The *Gaumont* The *Odeon* audiences would improve? More likely that with *Odeons* and *Gaumonts* closing all over the country, many becoming shops and offices, market forces were in full flight and The *Gaumont* site was just another financial deal.

Projection and technical information:

Kettering Electric Pavilion:

In 1913 when the *Kettering Electric Pavilion* opened there was a single Erneman mute projector and also one slide lantern of unknown make. The Erneman was a German projector but as films became longer, there was need for a second machine. The Erneman was replaced (date unknown, but it was during the anti-German feeling during the Great War) by two Ruffles Bioscopes which were made in Northampton. These were later replaced, again no actual date is known, but two Gaumont projectors (models not known, but possibly Chronos) and these two projectors were fitted with 'mirror-lite' arc lamps as the light source using eight inch mirrors. The projectors were to be changed yet again soon after, and replaced by two Cameragraphs.

The 1929 installation of sound involved a complete change of projection equipment. Two Simplex projectors with Cinephone sound heads were installed. A 33rpm BTH turntable was installed behind each projector. There were problems however with the installation, and in late 1930 it was removed. The replacement was with two Gaumont 16 projectors fitted with British Acoustic sound-on-film heads and British Acoustic amplification and Vulcan arc lamps. The sound-on-disc equipment was removed. Possibly this was updated to Kalee 7s or similar in later years.

The Gaumont:

The projection equipment was completely renewed with the refurbishment, and two Gaumont-Kalee 21s were installed with Westrex sound heads and amplification. These were the latest Kalee models and distinguishable by their square spool boxes. The light source was by Kalee arcs. It is thought that Delrama anamorphics were fitted for squeeze prints. The screen was fully masked for ratios between 1:75 to 1 and 2:35 to 1. Speakers were behind the screen and access to them may have been via the steel doors situated high on the back wall of the building facing Wadcroft.

Cinemascope prints shown would have been optical sound using names such as Perspecta. The cinema was exceptionally good for showing VistaVision prints. This was almost certainly because of the long shape of the auditorium which gave no 'sight-line' problems. The old cinema builders knew what they were doing.

THE EMPIRE

❁

THE NEW EMPIRE

❁

There will be few who can remember The *Empire* in Eskdail Street as it was. Today it is a motor repair centre, and the owners have even torn away its name *Empire Cinema* which for so many years remained proudly displayed high above its entrance, even after its demise. Though little remains of the original frontage now, the needs of the motor car have taken care of that, one can still see one or two features of the old cinema which had a special place in the cinema history of Kettering and which was left to die when it most needed its public.

It was in late 1919 when three enterprising Kettering businessmen laid plans and began the building of the town's second purpose built cinema. Mr H. G. Roughton, Mr A. Cheaney and Mr T. H. Bamford, who owned a photographic business in Montagu Street, formed a company and acquired land a short distance into Eskdail Street.

The building was quite simple being a basic hall with a pitched roof. The front was constructed out of brick, and with the exception of the entrance, was not particularly impressive. The entrance however, was to give the cinema its architectural 1920s character. It was in the form of a grand arch, the buttresses constructed in stone rising to the first parapet and decorated with Roman style regalia. The wide archway, forming the entrance, was ornately carved with similar patterns and the keystone bore an innocuous crest. Above the archway there were additional fanciful carvings.

Above the first parapet was an ornamental cornice and between them, the words EMPIRE CINEMA were inscribed in bold Roman capitals. A second parapet ran across the very top on which were three decorative roundels. In the early days each was adorned with an ornamental electric globe light. In the brickwork either side of the entrance were small windows, three high up and two below each side and between the two words of the cinema's name was the small projection room window.

Impression of how The Empire *looked in the 1920s.*

The outward appearance was typical of the modest and small purpose built cinemas of the day, which could be found in most towns the size of Kettering. Many of them were destined to become the local 'flea-pits' or 'bug-hutches' but The *Empire* could never have been in that category.

Internally it was a modest and comfortable cinema for the day. Entering through the splendid arch the small pay desk was reached by three short steps.

To each side were double doors leading to a small vestibule which ran the width of the building with stairs to the Balcony leading off from the left and right sides. It was quite small but served as access to the pay desk, toilets and a small door which led to a 'well' in which there was an iron ladder leading up into the projection room, which in reality was more of a 'box' than a room.

The auditorium was gained by double doors serving left and right aisles. The seating was tip-up red plush and raked. Crimson coloured walls were relieved by panels of white and cream, and lamps, which were described at the time as 'quaint looking', were set in them. The description of the new cinema is aptly given in a report from the *Kettering Leader* of Friday 7 May 1920.

'The opening of the Empire

> In attendance were the three owners of the Empire, Mr. H. G. Roughton, Mr. A. Cheaney and Mr. T. Bamford. All these gentlemen are well known for good business and acumen. The Empire looks good to begin with and has started life well. A wide, gracefully proportioned archway, of artistically formed stonework and decoration renders it very pleasing indeed. The interior of the theatre is nobly appointed. Seated throughout with tip-up seats upholstered in red plush and numbering between five and six hundred it is artistically decorated as well as being warmed and aired as may be required by means of methods up-to-date. The auditorium is a particularly pleasant place to spend a couple of hours or so.
>
> Among the features specially of note is the sufficiency of air space according to the season of the year. The means with the view to diffusing the light of the main electrics overhead are pleasingly effective. Attached to the walls are quaint looking lamps reminiscent of designs more in vogue with ones of a century or two ago. In the matter of technical equipment the Empire has the last word in projectors by means of which the pictures are displayed in a most perfect manner. With the latest and best films showing there is no need to wonder at the sure success which is attending Kettering's new picture house.'

The Balcony was small and in later years was to become perhaps the most popular place of any cinema in town. It had double seats described as 'hugging hutches'.

The *Empire* opened on Monday 3 May 1920 with the following programme:

Main Feature: Monday to Saturday throughout
Still Alarm (1919) starring Jack Manley and Betty Fordham

Supporting Feature:	Monday to Wednesday	*The Stars as they Were*
		Jerry Victory
		His Parlours Zoo
		Topical Budget
	Thursday to Saturday	*A Slate at Sea*
		One Round O'Brien
		Topical Budget

The opening was a great success as the review in the following day's *Evening Telegraph* suggests:

> 'Kettering's new cinema the Empire, opened on Monday to two crowded houses and the programme presented at this fine building was entirely worthy of their support. "Still Alarm", the story of a heroic fireman who became entangled with the schemes of a rogue has one of the most thrilling final scenes ever screened, when having set fire to his partners house, he discovers the heroine is shut in the burning building. This great melodrama is showing all week. Mention must be made of the efficient orchestra which contributed to the success of last nights entertainment.'

The programme for the following week, Monday 10 May, was *Daddy Long Legs* starring Mary Pickford and Mahlon Hamilton, supported by *Tommy Atkins in Berlin*, a Great War documentary, and it set the trend for showing quality pictures which continued for many years.

The success of The *Empire* was almost certainly the main reason for the demise of The *Hippodrome*. It had a Bijou Orchestra regularly playing for the films as well as providing musical interludes, comprising piano and violin for the lesser films, augmented by a bass, a cornet and a cello for the more prestigious showings, such as *Still Alarm* mentioned above. Hardly an orchestra by numbers, but nevertheless a very competent combination by all accounts, though quite where they all sat in such a small auditorium one can only guess.

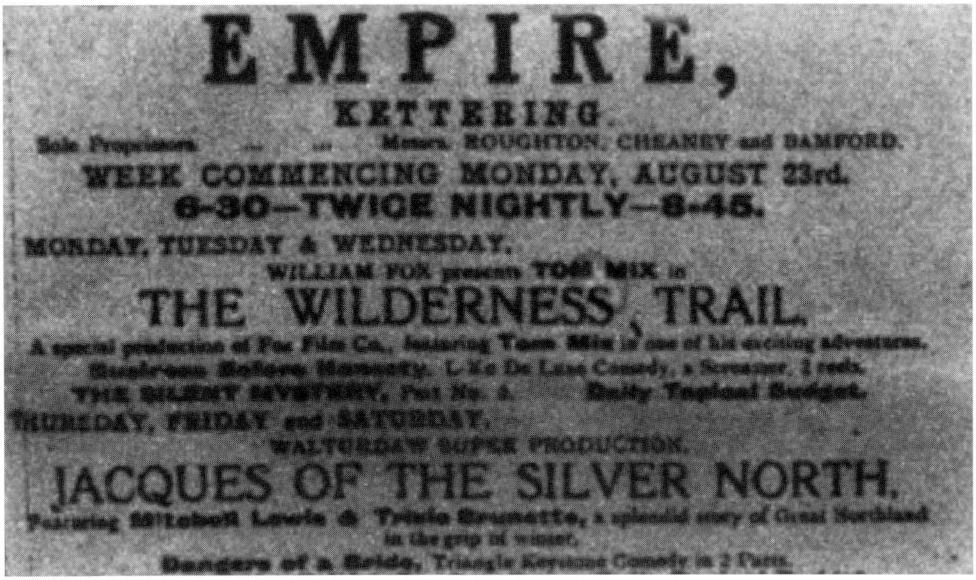

Typical August fare, 1920

The prices of admission at this time were Stalls 5d, 9d and 1s. The Balcony seats were 1s 3d. An additional price of 3d for Stalls was added later.

The *Empire* was quite late with the installation of' talkie' equipment. The work took place over four days in May 1931. The last silent programme to show was at the beginning of that week on Monday 4 May with *Venus* (aka *Venus of Venice*) (1927) starring Constance Talmadge supported by *Should A Mason Tell*. It would seem that The *Empire* had continued with silents until there were virtually none left. The proprietor, presumably, Bamford, stating that 'I am giving up silent films because it is no longer possible to get silents up to The *Empire* standard. The lack of silent films is forcing the change'.

It is undeniable that the paucity of silent films would have been reason enough for the change as the studios had gone over to 'talkies' entirely by 1930, except for Chaplin, but the real reason must have been lack of patrons at The *Empire*. The other cinemas had gone over to 'talkies' and the public loved them. Simply no one was interested in old silent films any more.

'Talkies' opened at The *Empire* on Monday 11 May 1931 (eighteen months after The *Pavilion*) with *Let Us Be Gay* (1930) starring Norma Shearer. An announcement for the changeover was publicised in the *Evening Telegraph* of Tuesday 5 May:

> **'First talkie at the Empire.**
> It is another talkie victory as the last of the silent cinemas in Kettering changes over. The last silent film programme that Kettering audiences will have an opportunity of seeing is being shown for the first three days of this week. On Thursday the Kettering Empire closes down whilst 'talkie' equipment is installed. The apparatus is of British Acoustic machines supplied by Gaumont and is of the very latest type being run entirely from the mains and not from batteries as formerly. This very latest equipment is brand new, the first of its kind going to Italy and the second coming to Kettering. The first talkie film to be shown will be "Let Us Be Gay" with Norma Shearer playing the lead role. Others booked are "The Unholy Three" with Lon Chaney, "Almost a Honeymoon" Dodo Watts, "Forward March" Buster Keaton and "Call of the Flesh" with Ramon Navaro. A new screen has been installed and it will be of the perforated type suited to new films.'

Thinking back, it must have been quite strange for those who had been regulars to this cinema suddenly to be confronted with sound from the screen. The lateness of the conversion had its advantages because the latest in 'talkie' amplification technology was to be installed in October of that year which provided the little cinema with the best sound in the county.

In 1937 The *Empire* changed hands and The *New Coliseum* owner, Jack Sherwood, added The *Empire* to his business. The *Empire* became the second-run cinema and therefore able to book virtually any film that had already shown at the town's circuit houses. It was inevitable that it also found an audience for the 'B' picture and it would often run a double bill of pictures with such stars as Hopalong Cassidy, Tom Mix and so on, and its programmes were almost always 'all action' pot boilers. I remember going to see *San Francisco* with my parents. I must have been about eight years old then. It had already been shown at The *Regal* and why we did not go there I guess was because The Empire was cheaper. I seem to remember my father booking the seats at the cycle shop on the corner of Montagu Street and Eskdail Street, Glover's I think it was. I was, I remember, awe-struck by the earthquake sequence in the film.

The *Empire* must have gone through other refurbishments. I remember maroon walls and the ceiling covered with pleated material. The proscenium was of a Grecian design and the tabs were maroon.

But the most notable feature of The *Empire* and the one that was most popular, at least with the boys and girls, was of course, the double seats in the Balcony. Called 'hugging hutches', you took you girl friend to The *Empire* to 'get better acquainted'. I wonder how many wedding bells the old *Empire* was responsible for? It was warm, comfortable and dark, and all for a few bob, half, if you went 'Dutch'.

The Empire *nearly always showed second run programmes – the circuit cinemas and the large independent having first call on the newly released films. However it did occasionally have first runs as these adverts show. It must be remembered that in those days cinemas had only one screen and so could not show all the pictures released in a given year, therefore the 'left overs' from the new releases were easy pickings for The Empire management, and so the pronouncement 'first time in Kettering' was proudly made. In later years all the cinema's adverts in the local press were set out in this format, though the 'block' adverts were also printed. Although 'block' adverts came about because of the paper saving requirements during the Second World War, they were slow to be phased out, these examples coming from 1946 and 1947* (Evening Telegraph)

After the Second World War, the fortunes of The *Empire* began to change, unhappily for the worse. It changed hands, this time to Mr Joseph Lee. In 1950, Mr H. D. Pascoe of Northampton took over the cinema and in May 1953 leased it to Mr W. H. Allcock who had previously run cinemas in Birmingham and Wolverhampton. By that time there had been a complete redecoration with up-to-date projection and sound equipment installed and the cinema received the modified name of The *New Empire*, but in little more than a year after Mr Allcock took over, the cinema closed.

In the post war years when the Manager was Joseph Lee, the staff included Mr Emmanuel Goldy, who had appeared in a different guise earlier in life at The *Regal*. The second projectionist was Bernard Ridley and Mr P. Cowan the third. In the final years of The *Empire*, Mr Cowan was the chief projectionist.

The shows were usually continuous from 5.30pm to about 10.30pm Mondays to Saturdays. There were also matinees on Thursday and Saturday, Thursday being the early-closing day in the town, starting at 2.30pm and running continuously until the end of the day. In later times, Sunday performances were at 7pm.

The final shows at the cinema commenced the week of Sunday 13 June 1954 and were: Sunday to Wednesday *Four Steps In The Clouds* (1942) starring Gino Servi, plus *The Chequered Coat* (1948) starring Tom Conway and Hurd Hatfield: Thursday to Saturday *Santa Fe* (1952) starring Randolph Scott, and *Captive Girl* (1953) with Johnny Weismuller

On Saturday night, 19 June 1954 at 10.30pm 'THE END' flashed on The *New Empire* screen for the very last time and the final episode in The *Empire* story was finished.

The New Empire *after closure. The facade more or less remains intact in this picture.*

It had been a popular house. It was not pretentious and showed the sort of programmes that always had an audience. The last three days were typical of its film far. So what went wrong?

William Allcock took over The *Empire* lease in May 1953. He had three other cinemas, two in Birmingham and one in Worcester. They were successful and under his management there was every reason to believe that The *Empire* would be also.

Allcock was no stranger to the cinema business. At the age of 16 he was one of the first operators to travel to remoter parts of the British Isles where permanent cinemas had not been, or would not be, established. His touring company included a substantial orchestra whose conductor was Paul Beard, father of the famous orchestra leader of the same name. Allcock was responsible for showing many of the famous silent classics, including *Birth of A Nation* (1915) and *Intolerance* (1916) which he had projected some 2,000 times.

With The *Empire* he took on a difficult ask. The circuit houses in the town took all the 'first runs' of pictures, and to compete, he chose to show the better continental films as strong supporting programmes to back up the second-run programmes which were only available at The *Empire*. 'For the first three days of "Behind Closed Doors (1953 French) we were packed out…then they never came again to see anymore' Allcock explained on closure.

One might say that this was the death knell of the old cinema. Perhaps Kettering was not a town where good continental films were acceptable or understood. The films were not low budget 'X' genre, but good products, however, Allcock, it seemed, fell victim to a patronage who voted with their feet and not with their heads.

Mr Allcock summed it up in a statement to the *Evening Telegraph* when The *New Empire* was closing:

> 'I have done everything to save the Eskdail Street house, I booked the right films and had a fair run of the best Continentals I don't know what the trouble was. This is a family hall and we made a speciality of giving patrons special attention but it seems that they are inclined to go out of town for their entertainment. My other cinemas are successful but in order to compete with the three circuit cinemas in Kettering I had to give the public something different. I chose to show continental films and backed them with strong supporting features.'

The building today. Some of the original features remain but the name has been removed....and oh, that roof!

The *Empire* was the second cinema to close in Kettering, the first being The *Hippodrome* 34 years earlier. It was the beginning of a spate of closures which were to follow until the town was, for a time, bereft of any cinema. Over the years, The *Empire* had been quite unfairly called a 'flea-pit'. It never was such, nor had it ever been. The *Empire* did not die because of unwarranted branding, property deals or boardroom decisions. It died simply because the public of Kettering left it to do so. Had they continued to support the little cinema, who knows it might have managed to survive and could have become good preservation potential with some sort of Community framework. Unfortunately nothing remains now to link the building with its past – not even its name up there on the parapet for all to see.

Projection and technical information:

When The *Empire* opened in 1920 the projectors installed were two mute Becks and one slide lantern. In 1931 sound was installed and the projectors were replaced with two Gaumont-Kalee 7s with British Acoustic sound heads and amplification.

In 1937 the sound equipment was replaced with British Acoustic Durosonic. New speakers were also installed behind the screen consisting of a treble horn and bass chamber. The treble horn was in fact a series of smaller horns, each perfectly matched, arranged in such a way that the sound was 'sprayed' over the audience.

In the final refurbishment of the cinema about 1950 the two Kalee 7s were replaced with Kalee 21s. It is not thought that wide screen was ever shown, although it may have been in the final year, but records are scarce on this point.

The projection room was very small indeed and by today's standards was a positive hazard. Arrived at by the iron ladder in the vestibule this was also the only way out and contact with the outside air and light was through the small vestibule window visible between the words EMPIRE and CINEMA on the façade. The film transit boxes had to be hauled up to the projection room for spooling up.

No details exist as to when screens were actually installed but obviously with the sound installation a new screen was required. Another, the last, was installed in the 1950's refurbishment. This is known because I was able to acquire material from it to construct a screen for the stage of the Working Men's Club in 1952 (see part 4).

There is reference to the original Becks obtaining their power from a battery source, but in 1931, with the conversion to sound, it required connection to the mains supply. Unfortunately research has so far failed to reveal what generative equipment would have been used previously. With battery operation, re-charging would have been necessary, probably daily, and this could only have been accomplished either from using a gas engine, the location of which is obscure, or for some other generative source. Many cinemas in those days used gas engines to generate their power source and so this is most likely the case with The *Empire*.

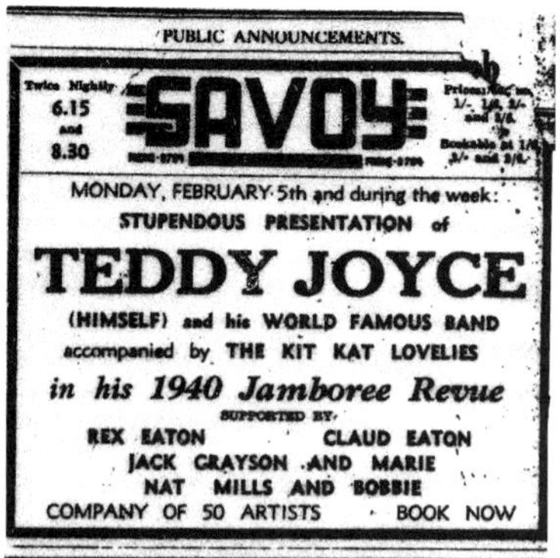

Pre Second World War press adverts (Evening Telegraph)

Press adverts, during the Second World War, mixing 'block' adverts with large ones. For some unknown reason this advert, dated 1942, refers to the Kettering Electric Pavilion *which had changed its name to the* Gaumont Pavilion *some 15 years earlier* (Evening Telegraph)

ODEON and PAVILION 1948

Press adverts from 1948 (Evening Telegraph)

April 1948.... This programming was really 'Something to shout about'....

More press adverts (Evening Telegraph)

THE REGAL

THE GRANADA

The owners of this new cinema have a reputation of owning some of the finest provincial cinemas in the country. The *Regal* is the finest of them all.' So said the publicity issued just prior to the opening of the new super-cinema under construction in the High Street in 1936. For once publicity was no exaggeration. Super-cinemas were in vogue. Large palaces built to match the importance of showing pictures to the masses in the style and grandeur of the 'movies' themselves.

Modern architecture and luxury provided the likes never before enjoyed by the working classes. Temples dedicated to the motion picture were erected in cities and towns, many of which still exist today, though sadly in different guises, as fine examples of 1930s design and architecture. The Kettering *Regal* was no exception.

It is difficult now to imagine what impact this huge building was making on the High Street, as it seemed to reach ever higher swamping the modest buildings around it. The construction started in 1935 on the site of Messrs Goosey and Sons, a drapery and fancy goods shop of some note in the area. It is not known how the site was acquired but it was of considerable size running so far back as to require another site to be cleared facing on to Gas Street (now Meadow Road). The design was by George Coles of London, and the builders were Henry Kent, also of London. The owners, Cohen and Rafler, owned other cinemas in the provinces and London, one being The *Ritz* at Southend. It cost £70,000 to build The *Regal*.

The Goosey and Sons fancy goods store in the High Street which was demolished to make way for The Regal

OLD LANDMARK BEING DEMOLISHED.

Kettering Shops Making Way for Luxury Cinema.

A SUPER CINEMA ACCOMMODATING 2000 PERSONS WITH CAR PARK FOR 100 CARS WILL BE ERECTED ON THIS SITE

LIKE MARIONETTES these workmen at the top of the building give a picturesque touch to this "Kettering Leader" picture of an early stage in the process of demolition.

Workmen are already busy demolishing property in High-street, Kettering, to make way for a new £70,000 super-cinema which will seat 2,000 people.

Formerly the property of Messrs. Goosey and Son, the oldest drapery firm in Kettering, the buildings are on the western side of High-street and occupy one of the chief positions.

The new cinema, which it is hoped will open in September, will be built by Messrs. Cohen and Rafer, of London, and will be on the latest lines, in fact a West End house in miniature.

Its provisional name is "The Savoy," and from end to end of the 80 feet frontage it is planned to have swing doors and above them long narrow windows.

Balconies to seat nearly 800 will be provided, and the stalls, on the street level will hold nearly 1,200. Provisions for an orchestra, organ and car park are being [illegible]

[illegible] of the shops and yard [illegible] occupied by an entrance [illegible] which will avoid the [illegible] Patrons will be [illegible] covered by [illegible]

Relic of the days when the property was a mansion, this fine 18th century oak staircase with its twisted balusters has been dismantled. Apart from the damage caused by its removal, the staircase is in almost perfect condition.

Notice for The Regal *construction on the front of Goosey's shop* (Evening Telegraph)

I remember distinctly the large board fronting the scaffold in the High Street which proclaimed the building of a large new super-cinema. I could only have been seven years old at the time, and it is strange how that stays in the mind. It was certainly the beginnings of an affection I was to have for the cinema which was to see me working in the building later in life, and which today still provides me with happy and treasured memories.

The front of The *Regal* was quite unusual in its design and said to be the only one of its kind in the whole of Europe. The front, dominated by the tower rising high above the street and topped with a 'mushroom' is with us still and when lit with its neon light made a giant halo. It could be seen many miles away especially from the heights of Broughton.

Sweeping away from each side of the tower were flanking walls which joined up to the two massive buttresses forming the bulk of the frontage. The impressive tower had a tall thick glazed 'window' which was illuminated at night from behind with strips of neon changing colours continually. Outlining the front were more neon strips. The large canopy provided a letterbox for advertising the current films and above, in big single letters, was the name REGAL which was also illuminated. Though the neon display would be short lived, because of the troubled times just ahead, whilst it existed it was a beautiful sight and I remember watching in fascination as the lights changed through the colour spectrum. It was the focal point of the High Street.

Inside, the cinema was even more impressive. The five pairs of entrance doors led into a large foyer with a pay desk each side, and then another set of similar doors led into the magnificent vestibule. The two pay desks were used at busy times during the weekends and holidays. The left hand pay desk was for the Circle seats and the right for the Stalls. At other times the right side was used for all seats.

Display and sales were also in the foyer. The vestibule was spacious, and to the left a large plated mirror rose up the centre of the wall to the frieze which surrounded three sides, and bore an attractive wavy pattern mirror, which was draped with silk material. Ahead there were steps down to another vestibule which contained services such as toilets and the Manager's office and so on, before leading directly into the capacious auditorium.

The main vestibule was lavishly furnished with two large luxury divans back-to-back in the centre, and reaching down from the roof was a large central light fitting in the cinema's lighting style. The ceiling was designed with sunken panels. The main vestibule had, many uses and exhibitions were often staged there. During the Second World War, I remember a full-sized cockpit of a Spitfire being displayed for 'Spitfire Week' and again a large display of Naval fighting equipment and a mock-up of a ship's bridge for 'Warship Week'. Many other similar displays were staged in this vestibule and of course, there was always something on display about the forthcoming pictures. It was lavished with potted palms and exotic plants which gave an air of elegance and opulence.

Either side of the steps rose two large supporting pillars which were hollow at first floor level. Each side of these were modern grand stairs leading to an upper terrace area which was used as a restaurant. At that level each of the pillars served a useful role – one was a telephone kiosk, and the other the restaurant office.

At the far end of the restaurant were two sets of doors. Beyond the left-side doors was an exit flight of steps from the Rear Circle. This was also the way to the projection room. During the time I worked in the building I got to know each one of those steps when loaded up with the metal boxes containing film programmes, I struggled up to the Box.

The right hand set of doors led patrons to a small vestibule which contained the entrances to the toilets. A short flight of stairs then led to the centre cross-aisle of the massive Circle, where the four blocks down towards the front gave the best view.

The auditorium was very modern. The ceiling was a series of 'stepped' levels reaching the wide curved proscenium. Concealed lighting panels ran the length of the ceiling with plain opal glass suspended over scrolled metalwork. In the Stalls, the overhanging Circle ceiling was decorated with three large roundels which served as air circulating ducts. Here, as with the lighting throughout the cinema, light fittings were opal glass and metal scroll. Between each stepped portion of the ceiling a decorative plasterwork pattern ran to the side and then down the wall, each having a large ornamental wall light as part of the auditorium lighting.

Whilst the vestibule was decorated in shades of pink, the auditorium was in shades of buff. The proscenium arch was a modern plasterwork design with fluted bands running horizontally every few feet around the arch. Behind this plasterwork arch was three-colour lighting which changed constantly.

There was an orchestra pit but no under-stage entrance. Each side of the stage were small display levels, which, in the early days, contained decorative foliage. During the Second World War the right hand side contained a display which when illuminated, would advise patrons of an 'air raid warning'.

The stage was quite large, a little under 50 feet wide, and had a curved apron front, which as well as containing footlights, was spacious enough to be used for acts to take place in front of the tabs. The screen was on the back wall. Behind the screen was the speaker chamber, its entrance gained from the rear of the building.

There were three sets of tabs, though other sets could be fitted up. The screen tabs were silver in colour and were conventionally opened. Between these and the front tabs was a set so unique that only a few of its type were ever installed. It was a festooned drop curtain, or contour curtain, which was a new device in stage equipment at that time. The curtain could be 'festooned' into 59 different shapes or designs which could either be set to a pattern or to change automatically. It took five minutes to complete the cycle and then start anew when programmed to automatic.

Back stage, there were four dressing rooms and staff rooms. The new cinema was equipped with the latest 'air washing' system keeping the atmosphere inside always fresh with clean air, and the projection equipment installed was of the highest standard.

In later years when I worked in the cinema, often, when it was empty, I would stand with my back to the orchestra pit rail and look up to the back wall of the Circle. This view was impressive, showing the real size of the auditorium and its magnificence. From the stage it was even more impressive and one can easily understand why bands and artists loved to perform at The *Regal*. Using a preview support from the *Kettering Leader* dated Friday 11 December 1936, just two weeks before the opening, the importance of this new cinema's presence in the town can be appreciated:

> **'Modern Cinema Marvels**
> With the nearing completion of the Regal cinema at Kettering the term 'modern cinema marvels' could be an appropriate description of the new Kettering super-cinema which is to be opened shortly. Up-to-date, magnificent and modern in every way it is a veritable hall of wonders. As a luxury cinema it is one of the finest in the provinces and money has not been spared in fitting it out. The best of everything has been initiated to make the Regal in many ways a unique theatre with its own particular niche in cinema history.
>
> The unusual front with its tall and dignified tower, flanked each side with massive buttresses has completely altered the appearance of the High Street. Its construction has been watched with great interest. The tower will be illuminated with the newest neon lighting equipment which will change from pale blue down to pale pink. Inside the tower hidden away behind thick glass are perpendicular neon strips which are illuminated alternately in the different colours to give this effect.
>
> The interior of the cinema has the air circulated with modern equipment. The air is drawn in to the cinema first passing through

this equipment where it is washed and purified before being circulated throughout the building. For showing the films the finest equipment has been obtained and installed. The arc lamps have been brought into Britain especially and the latest devices for the protection of the patrons has been installed.'

The sumptuous and vast stalls are of the auditorium. The beautiful festooned curtain can be seen draped in one of its 59 possible patterns (Winfield)

The super-cinema opened on Boxing Day Saturday 26 December 1936 amid tremendous razzle-dazzle. The published programme for the opening is reconstructed here and every one of the near 2,000 seats, splendid grey in the Stalls and 'fitted' blue in the Circle, was filled.

REGAL
SUPER CINEMA
CAR PARK KETTERING CAFÉ

GRAND OPENING CEREMONY
By the R. H. Earl Spencer DL
Boxing Day Saturday December 26th 1936 at 8pm

Prelude and Overture by
MUNN AND FELTONS WORKS BAND
Fanfare:
THE HERALD TRUMPETERS
Opening Address and Ceremony by the R. H. Earl Spencer DL
And the Chairman of Kettering Urban District Council
Followed by an address by Mr. L. Morely-Clarke, Manager

On The Screen
Ivor Morton and Dave Kaye with Harry Roy and his Band in
"EVERYTHING IS RHYTHYM"
and "Building a Building"
"Audioscopix" in 3-D
On The Stage
PETULENGRO and his Ladies Hussar Broadcasting Band
*
For the REGALS Big Broadcast tune in to RADIO NORMANDIE on Christmas day at 2.30pm.

The broadcast on Radio Normandie was apparently a pre-opening ‘commercial’ and the first time locally such a method was used to advertise an event of this nature. Little detail exists but reports suggest that the story of the new cinema, its opening the next day, and a snippet from the track of *Everything is Rhythm* comprised the air slot.

Although there was no celebrity from the world of cinema attending the opening, there were crowds in the High Street taking in the atmosphere of the prestigious event. The *Regal* shone like the glittering jewel that it was, its neon lighting up the street in shades of blues, yellows and reds, the edges of the building glimmering in the strips of coloured light, with the mushroomed top of the tower lit with a blue-ish tint atop the flood lighting. It was the best Christmas decoration that the town had probably seen and it would be there night after night from then on.

A review of the opening night appeared in the *Evening Telegraph*:

> 'The Regal Kettering, the towns new 2000 seat super-cinema was declared open on Boxing day before a full audience. Built on the most modern lines the Regal has a striking façade reputed to be the only one of its kind in Europe. Besides providing first class entertainment it plays a large part in brightening the main street of the town.
>
> Munn and Feltons Works band filled out the orchestra pit providing an enjoyable musical programme before the opening ceremony. Four trumpeters heralded the opening ceremony and then Mr. Morely-Clarke, the General Manager, welcomed the audience from the stage saying that though Kettering had five cinemas now he pledged that the Regal would be able to offer a wider variety of entertainment which would include stage as well as screen.
>
> Then followed a film "Building a Building" which told the story of the building of the Regal from its commencement to its completion and it sparkled with the humour provided by the workers involved. Spectacles with red and green eyepieces, issued to all patrons on entering, were donned to see "Audioscopix" [*which was an MGM Pete Smith speciality short film in the 3-D anaglyph system*] a hilarious little picture filmed in the third dimension. The official opening then took place by the R. H. Earl Spencer followed by an address by the Chairman of the Council. There then followed the entertaining film "Everything Is Rhythm" starring Harry Roy and his Band. The evening came to a close with a delightful concert by Petulengro and his Ladies Hussar band.'

That programme ran for the whole of the following week. The week after that saw The *Regal* getting down to the business of drawing its patrons, and lined up was the first showing in Kettering of *Queen of Hearts* starring the very popular Gracie Fields.

The cinema soon began its Sunday evening celebrity concerts which were to be the hallmark of excellent entertainment, people travelling from all parts of the county to attend them. Top bands of the day appeared on its stage

The High Street with The Regal, *1939* (D. Wharton)

including Joe Loss, Jack Hylton, Geraldo, Ambrose, Henry Hall, and many others. Anyone who remembers these concerts will recall the visit by Nat Gonella in May 1939 when the Band had a standing ovation and repeated encores. The pianists Rawicz and Landaur appeared on a number of occasions, as did singers Anne Zeigler and Webster Booth. It is said that Reginald Foorte played at The *Regal*, but The *Savoy* visit in 1940 seems to be his only recorded visit to the town.

The beloved Flanagan and Allan appeared, as did the Oscar Rabin Band, and throughout the War, hosts of popular stars of stage and radio. The concert by Ambrose and his Orchestra featured the band's leading female vocalist, Vera Lynn, soon to gain immortality as the 'Forces' Sweetheart'. The celebrity concerts continued throughout the War years, but were interspersed with the 'hostilities only' Sunday film programmes right up until 1947.

Some of the greatest films of the 1930s and 1940s were screened at The *Regal*. *Gone With The Wind* played for two weeks, which was very unusual in a provincial town in those days, only to return by popular demand shortly afterwards. People were queuing along the High Street and down Gas Street (Meadow Road). I remember seeing this film with my parents and I cannot recollect if I actually understood it then, but the important thing is that I saw it the first time round. I saw other great films there including *Mutiny On The*

REGAL
COMING ATTRACTIONS

TWO WEEKS YOU MUST NOT MISS !

JULY 19th.

COLOSSAL AMATEUR TALENT PRESENTATION WEEK

ALSO 2 FEATURE FILMS.

JULY 26th

ANOTHER STUPENDOUS STAGE SHOW

KETTERING'S FIRST CRAZY WEEK.

AND FULL FILM PROGRAMME.

REGAL CAFE

For

MORNING COFFEE

1/6 4 COURSE LUNCHEON 1/6

DAINTY TEAS

1/- CINEMA SUPPERS 1/-

LIGHT REFRESHMENTS

VARIETY EACH WEEK

AT EVERY PERFORMANCE

R-E-G-A-L

General Manager: L. MORLEY CLARKE.

KETTERING

Sunday Variety CONCERT

Sunday, 20th June, 1937

PROGRAMME 2D.

JOHN S. PIKE, PRINTER, CANON ST., KETTERING.

Programme

MRS.

JACK HYLTON

WITH HER BOYS

Mrs. Jack Hylton and her Boys will play a Selection from the following :—

1 Sing Baby Sing
2 Serenade in the Night
3 Our Hyltonisms
4 Did Your Mother Come from Ireland
5 Sailor Where Art Thou
6 Marguerita
7 Waltz in Swing Time
8 Lollipop Shop
9 There's a New World
10 Au Revoir
11 Medley of Popular Songs
12 Did You Mean It
13 Fleet's in Port Again
14 Old Favourite Selection
15 Memories from 1924—1928
16 Tiger Rag
17 Rhythm Saved the World
18 Hot Medley
19 Gershwin Medley
20 A Song That Goes Like This
21 When The Poppies Bloom Again
22 Let's take a stroll around the Park
23 Golfing
24 Chapel in the Moonlight
25 I'm an Old Cowhand
26 I'll sing you a thousand love songs
27 Dinah
28 Laughing Irish Eyes
29 When My Dream Boat Comes Home
30 You've got a go "Left! Right!"
31 When the Sun says Good-night to the Mountain
32 Love Medley
33 Rumba
34 Medley of Old Rhythm Numbers
35 Easy to Love
36 Memory of a Tiny Shoe
37 Sing, Sing, Sing
38 Good-night My Love
39 Alone in Vienna

Arrangers—Billy Ternent, Len Edwards and John Bristol

Challen Grand Piano—
Supplied by Alf Bailey, Gold Street, Kettering.

THIS IS THE MISSUS.

Business Woman, Financial Expert, Airwoman and Artist.

Ennis (Mrs. Jack) Hylton . . . .

Petite. Naturally blonde. Formerly Ennis Parkes, soubrette.

Supervises everything in connection with her band, including bookings, supplementary acts, and fan mail, which runs into several hundreds of letters a week. People write to her from all parts of the world ; estimated yearly cost of supplying them with autograph pictures, etc., is in the region of £500.

Here's a letter Ennis received recently.

"dere madam, mi littel alfred is a rare one on the cornit please send £20 his father sed it wil be orl rite . ."

Many letters requesting signed pictures come from patients in hospitals. No one is ever refused. Mrs, Jack is tremendously proud of these admirers,

Every minute outside theatre, dance and concert hall is devoted to her public. Opening charity bazaars, judging beauty contests, attending functions.

Occasionally, about once every six months, she spends a quiet week at home. The Hylton house is in Mayfair...a queer little house. Certainly one of the most original in London.

Planned and furnished by Ennis, they call it "The House That Mrs. Jack Built." It incorporates, amongst other suprising features, an underground sound-proof music hall wherein an entire band can rehearse without disturbing the neighbours. There's a whoopee room, with bagatelle board, dart board (autographed), houp-la, and a cocktail bar where Ennis will mix you a "J.H. Special"

Says Ennis about women. They don't dress to please men. They dress to make other women talk.

Her favourite dish is bacon and eggs ; her favourite quotation the Christian Science movement motto "Things and people are only as important as you choose to make them." Is an enthusiastic airwoman. Inaugurated the Humber air ferry last year, and, along with her husband, was the first person to fly from London to Deauville.

NEXT CONCERT — SUNDAY 4th JULY.

One of the Sunday concerts (J. Filby)

Bounty (1939), *Wizard Of Oz* (1939) and so many others. Humphrey Bogart was my hero and Bette Davis my favourite actress, and most of their pictures were shown here.

I remember The *Regal* as being my 'palace' and I could be found in the cinema every week, twice if it was a split week. As a lad, I would visit all of Kettering's cinemas most weeks, but The *Regal* was my favourite. I would often dream of getting in to that projection room and show the pictures. Little did I know that one day I actually would.

Seat prices for this luxury were very modest. Front Stalls 6d, Centre Stalls 9d, Rear Stalls 1s, Rear Circle 1s 6d, Front Stalls 2s. For the Sunday concerts the seats were priced at 6d, 1s, 1s 6d, 2s and 2s.6d. By 1946 the prices, though increased, were still very reasonable for a cinema of this calibre: Front Stalls 10d, Centre Stalls 1s, Rear Stalls 1s 9d, Rear Circle 2s 3d and Front Circle 2s9d.

The Regal *was famed for its Sunday celebrity concerts* (Evening Telegraph)

After the Second World War there were moves to acquire the cinema by the Essoldo chain. However towards the end of 1947, negotiations took place between the owners and Granada Theatres Limited, a London based cinema circuit, with theatres in the Home Counties and Midlands.

This staff photograph was taken in November 1946. Jack Goldy the manager, is second row centre; Manny Goldy, extreme left; Eric Walters, chief projectionist, is forth right on the same row.

From Thursday 1 January 1948, Granada Theatres took over The *Regal* and re-named it The *Granada*. The splendid neon display, blacked out all through the War, was revived as soon as restrictions were lifted, but the ravages of weather and lack of maintenance had reduced its effect, and with the change of ownership it was never returned to its former spectacle, and a part of the old *Regal* had disappeared for ever.

The last show as The *Regal* was *Quiet Wedding* (1940) starring Margaret Lockwood and Derek Farr, and supporting was *Broadway* (1942) with George Raft.

Two interesting items are left as mysteries about The *Regal.* In the plans there was to have been a Wurlitzer organ installed, but it never happened, and why was the proposed name of *Savoy* changed to *Regal*? These mysteries may never be solved, but one thing is for sure, there was no other cinema like it in the county. It was indeed a 'peoples' palace'.

'*Granada* stands as the word guaranteeing intimate comfort, good programmes and service with a smile'. That was the pledge made when the new Manager, Mr W. Bush, arrived at The *Granada* in the first week of 1948. The process of 'Granada-ising' the old *Regal* had begun.

The real task was the actual changeover, for old names and friends die hard. For Mr Bush it was not made any easier by not having any redecoration or even a break between the change. The cinema did not close, as it did not need any refurbishment, apart from the change of the main sign and some slight cosmetic work inside.

After The Granada *conversion*
(Photo Coverage)

An advert appeared in the local paper saying quite simply '~~REGAL~~ GRANADA. Begin saying GRAH-NAH-DAH'. This was reinforced by the removal of the REGAL name over the canopy and the erection of an illuminated sign on the buttress adjoining the Midland Bank displaying the word GRANADA in the Company's corporate logo.

From the first day the staff were turned out in new uniforms. Blue suits and peaked caps for the men, dark blue skirts, gold satin blouses and chic hats for the ladies. New internal display boards, corporate lettering and necessary cosmetic decorating, added to the new look, enhancing the new image. On the screen new Granada-style day sets and logos appeared and corporate style of film presentation was the order of the day.

The impressive Granada *vestibule (*Photo Coverage*)*

Granada Theatres were run by the Bernstein family. It was a relatively small circuit until after the Second World War when it began to buy up cinemas mainly the south, but extended its business as far as Grantham and Oswestry. Both Cecil and Sidney Bernstein were fully active in the business and ran the cinemas to a very high standard. The *Granada* at Tooting, their 'flagship', was an elaborate place and held as an example to all the other 80 or so cinemas in the circuit. The cinema at Kettering would benefit for many years by being part of this circuit.

The first programme to show in The *Granada* was on Monday 4 January 1948 being *Squadron Leader X* (1942) starring Eric Portman and Ann Dvorak. The programmes for a while, according to the advertisements, were frequently second-run films but eventually the Associated British-Pathe films, Warner Brothers and MGM productions and independent film companies were booked in for first runs.

The Sunday celebrity concerts seemed to have continued but there are no records of bookings apart from occasional concerts given by local artists and bands – live entertainment was far from regular. There were stage performances later when the upsurge of popular music was such that local bands were springing up all over the place, and during the Sunday film performances the better ones were booked for 30 minutes slots.

At the beginning of the 1950s The *Granada* underwent refurbishment. It was mainly cosmetic and done without closure. For weeks, audiences would see tall scaffolding within the auditorium and elsewhere, the work being accomplished by working through the nights and sometimes only finishing minutes before the afternoon performances. The colour schemes were bold and exciting, with red, blues, blacks, gold and other shades.

The lighting was totally changed with a large electrolier suspended high above the Stalls, and small ones under the Circle. Constructed in gilded metalwork and opal glass, these electroliers had to be dropped and cleaned frequently. Oh, how I remember going up into the false ceiling and winding down the big electrolier. When helping to do this I was always mindful of the *Phantom Of The Opera* (the 1942 Claude Rains version) and fancied myself with a hacksaw. It was a complete morning's work for all the projection staff and how many 60 watt bulbs (or were they 100 watt?) were needed to replace every one of the lights. I fail to remember.

The proscenium was remodelled with a false arch fitted over the original. It was finished in a mottled blue-grey with a gilt surround around each edge. Whilst it was impressive I would have preferred the original to have remained. I always felt that something uniquely aesthetic was lost by covering the old *Regal* proscenium. The remainder of the building was also decorated in the bold colours the Granada group seemed to like so much. It certainly did give a luxurious look and feel to the cinema.

The two pay desks were reduced to one only, that being on the left side of the foyer, and the right side was converted in to a cafeteria and snack bar. The two settees were to go, as were the potted palms, though these may have already been removed earlier. The overall effect was one of retained luxury and modernity.

The *Granada* was perhaps at its height of popularity at this time. Many of the prestigious pictures and all of the MGM musicals played there. In 1954 there were two events of note. The first saw the cinema showing three-dimensional films. The fight to survive the impact of television brought out new and innovative ideas from the big studios, and Warner Brothers, taking the initiative, following the success of the United Artists *Bwana Devil* (1952) in NaturalVision, came out with *House Of Wax* (1953) in NaturalVision, starring Vincent Price. This film opened a series of 3-D films at The *Granada*.

NaturalVision 3-D was totally different to the 'anaglyph' system shown on the opening night of The *Regal* back in 1936. Whilst spectacles still had to be worn, they resembled sun glasses and the image was quite spectacular. To project 3-D, a special projection synchronising unit toured the *Granada* cinemas selected to show them. With this unit also came a stereophonic sound integrator which provided sound effects.

The second innovation came from Twentieth Century Fox. It was an 'anamorphic' system which when filmed by the camera squeezed the picture horizontally into the frame, and when projected, 'unsqueezed' the picture, giving a visual image on the screen of two and a half times the width to the height (magnetic prints only). The system was called Cinemascope with full four-track stereophonic sound.

Fox had to peddle this around a bit and, as I mentioned before, Rank would only install this new system in prestigious houses. The *Odeon* at Kettering was not one of these. Independents such as Granada, Essoldo and the like, were wooed by Fox to install full Cinemascope and The *Granada* at Kettering received its installation during September 1954. It was the whole works, with full four-track magnetic sound and a huge 52 feet wide by 20 feet high screen with variable masking. Behind this huge screen were three speaker installations, one each for left and right and one in the middle. Placed around the auditorium, Stalls and Circle, were ambient speaker sets to carry forth 'effects' tracks.

The first programme to be shown in this process, running for two weeks starting Monday 4 October 1954, was *The Robe* (1953) starring Victor Mature, Jean Simmons and Michael Rennie, with *Vesuvius Express*, and highlights of the Empire Games. It was an outstanding success and I can remember seeing queues round the High Street and down beyond the cinema car park in Meadow Road. Three performances each day, four on Saturday, the house records were broken and nothing like it was seen again until the *Sound Of Music.*

*The Granada staff Christmas party, early 1950s (*Evening Telegraph*)*

*...and equally festive (*Evening Telegraph*)*

I recollect the first days of *The Robe* showings. When the curtains were opened, the screen masking had already opened to Cinemascope behind them, the audiences were somewhat awe-struck by the picture presented to them. It stretched for one side of the stage to the other, some 50 feet of it, which was two and a half times wide as it was high. The gasps and comments in the otherwise hushed auditorium expressed the reaction.

For The *Granada* the next hugely popular period was the series of 'pop-package' one-night shows which were staged from the late 1950s through to the 1960s. Just about every British pop star of the day appeared, plus some American ones as well. The shows were wild and very noisy and it is a credit to the builders that the building withstood the punishment, but withstand it it did, and it really rocked for regular two hour long performances. Nothing quite like those shows had ever been seen before in Kettering and certainly not since. Admission prices to these shows were 5s, 7s and 10s (you paid the most to be deafened the most) and you would queue for an hour even with a reservation. They were staged every few weeks and were tremendously received.

Uncle Jack gets his birthday card from The Kettering 'Granadiers' (J Filby)

The fortunes were to wane, however. In 1968 the 'Granadiers' Saturday morning children's club closed. In February 1974 the Stalls were closed and seating confined to the Circle only. It came as a shock when at the beginning of June the same year, Granada Theatres announced that the cinema was to close on Saturday 8 June 1974, and thus forty years of cinema in Kettering's most super house were to cease.

After a short closure the building was re-opened as a Bingo Club which can only be described as an inglorious end to a glorious life.

The last programme was a seven day run of *Zardoz* starring Sean Connery and Charlotte Rampling. Unfortunately this film did not help the sorrow of closing at all, as it was probably the worst film Connery had made up to then, and was described by one critic as a 'glittering cultural trash pile'. Stalwarts could hardly have left the cinema after that showing with anything less than dejection.

During the last showing on the Saturday night, the song 'So Long, Farewell' from the *Sound Of Music* was played. It may have been better to have shown that film as a farewell. At least it would have surely drawn a goodly attendance and been a fitting finale to the life of a 'modern cinema marvel'.

Although by now I was living elsewhere I could not feel but great sorrow when hearing that The *Granada* had closed. My associations with the building had reached back nearly to its beginnings and I felt a sense of losing what had been part of my life. Perhaps the words of two of the staff best epitomises the feelings experienced by those who were witness to the loss of a dearly loved cinema - a house of excellence that lived up to The *Regal* claim. 'Kettering people don't know what they want. No matter what shows we put on they are not even interested enough to find out what we are showing. It's a lovely building and a smashing cinema'. 'The new generation don't seem bothered with the cinema. The staff are very upset, and I have had my little cry'.

How poignant are those few last words.

THE END: Granada cinema closes

10 JAN 1974

THE staff of the Granada, Kettering, mourned the passing of their cinema when it closed down on Saturday night.

About 20 workers from the cinema were affected by the close down, although some will be given new jobs in other Granada cinemas.

Mrs Ann Beck (24) and Mrs Irene Heads are part-time cashiers who are now out of a job. Ann said: "I feel terrible. I have been here three years, and Irene for four."

Irene added: "Kettering people don't know what they want. No matter what shows we put on they were not interested enough even to find out what we were showing, let alone come along.

"People want to get away from home, and what else is there Only going to the pubs. It's a lovely building and a nice cinema.

"We have noticed an improvement this last week. There were more people coming in for a last visit.

"There was one woman in particular who came in every day for years. Two old couples were always there before we opened.

"There were quite a few who came every week no matter what, but not enough to keep us going.

"We had about a dozen regulars. Some of them were speechless when they heard the cinema was closing. They just did not know what to do.

"The afternoon cashier has been here 14 years. She is 67 and worked all her life in cinemas, first at the Gaumont, then the Odeon and then here. The kiosk manageress has been here 10 years."

Stuart Shepherd is a 20-year-old projectionist. He worked at the Granada five years. He said: "The usherettes have been very upset and I have had my little cry. The cinema was like your second home."

Commissionaire Harold Carpenter said: "I started at the cinema when it was the Regal and there used to be queues every night.

There is a new generation coming up who don't seem to be bothered with the cinema in Kettering."

How the closure was reported, and showing Stuart Shepherd threading the very last reel of film ever to be shown at The Granada, *which closed at 10.09pm that evening*

The façade as it is today. Thankfully it is a listed building, and therefore will be taken care of.

Projection and technical information:

The Regal:

The *Regal* was originally fitted out with two Ross FC1 projectors fitted with RCA Photophone sound heads. Amplification was also RCA. There was a slide projector, one follow-spot and a full twin-turntable non-synch unit. The projection room was very spacious. The stage lighting was controlled from a lighting board in the projection room, and was tri-colour. The tabs, including the festoon, were also controlled from the projection room. Ross arc lamps were the light source.

Some time later, the Ross FC1s were replaced with Ross GC1s though when this took place is not clear, but it might have been at the time off the Granada takeover. The screen was standard Academy ratio, and on the back wall, the sound chamber built out and was accessed from the rear of the theatre.

The Granada:

It would appear that the Ross projection equipment in place at the changeover from The *Regal* to The *Granada* remained so for many years, in fact right up until 1954. With the installation of Cinemascope a higher powered light source was required. I am sure, though unable to confirm in my mind, that this up-grading was installed for the 3-D presentations, however the old Ross arc lamps were replaced about this time by two Peerless Magnarc units which was a vast improvement over the originals.

With 3-D the two Ross GC1s were linked by a Selsync unit. The effects sound was obtained using a separate sound reproduction unit which was fed to the speakers installed around the auditorium. A special wide ratio 'Miraglo' screen was installed towards the front stage and was coated silver. The equipment, except the screen, was portable, and toured other Granada theatres. The system in use at that time required both projectors in use for separate left-hand and right-hand prints and linked by the Selsync unit. Polarisation filters were placed immediately before the respective projector lenses. The system was Polaroid natural Vision requiring personal polarisation spectacles to be worn by the viewer which resembled sunglasses to look at.

Cinemascope was installed using the Ross GC1s. the Peerless arc lamps have already been mentioned. Between the upper spool box and the projector head a type LMI 9010 RCA Magnetic sound head was fitted to each projector.

The sound head was 'self-drive' by which the film was pulled over a stabilizing drum and then across a four-track magnetic pick-up cluster. The optical sound head remained in position. Larger spool boxes became standard. The projection optical system was fitted with a standard 'backing lens' and a Kalee 'Varamorph' anamorphic lens fitted to each projector. The aperture plates for the different aspect ratios were manually set for each system use.

The RCA sound amplification system was increased for stereophonic sound using four pre-amplifiers to boost the magnetic track signals to levels comparable to optical track signals. From the pre-amps the signal was passed to three standard voltage amplifiers and then to the three two-way speakers behind the screen. A fourth amplifier supplied the 'effects' track signal, through the suppressor unit (to ensure evenly diffused sound) and then to the 24 ambient speakers around the auditorium. Change-over to/from magnetic or optical was by a photo-magnetic switch.

The screen was 52 feet wide and 20 feet high and was curved. Installed forward of the back wall of the stage, it was mounted on a tubular frame and was installed to allow room for stage presentations. Full motorised screen masking to all ratios was available.

Later, the actual date is not recorded, the system was changed to two Philips projectors and Westrex sound. For stage shows the special amplification and huge speaker cabinets were brought in.

THE ODEON 8-SCREEN MULTIPLEX

❀

Nestled in a corner of the Kettering Retail Park, and by the A14 link road, is Pegasus Court. An apt name perhaps for it is here that can be found the latest example of a temple for the showing the wonder and mystique of motion pictures. The *Odeon* 8-Screen Multiplex provides a choice of all the latest films in a 'state-of-the-art' environment.

The *Odeon* is an extremely pleasant and well designed building, which is more than can be said for many Multiplexes around the country, and manages to retain that special luxury feeling of a super-cinema from the past.

It was in 1995 that the first rumblings were heard for the building of a multiplex at Kettering. Competition from sites at Wellingborough and Corby and elsewhere threatened Kettering into becoming a cinematic wilderness. Because of lack of support for The *Ohio* the latest films could not be booked into those two screens and therefore to see them, when first released, it required travel to Milton Keynes, Northampton or even Peterborough. Only a few stalwart supporters, and those lacking mobility, visited The *Ohio* and the mobile young were not interested in the remaining cinemas.

In 1996 news was forthcoming that the Kettering site had finally been chosen and building would start. However, there was some delay and the construction became behind schedule.

The cinema is built on a site having also received restaurant and pub facilities as well as shopping services, all with ample car parking. Its potential is enormous, having both a large urbanised area nearby, and good access by public and private transport. The developers, Farrho Developments, along with Rank Leisure, owners of the Multiplex, completed the work in December 1997.

The *Odeon* 8-screen Multiplex opened with an extravaganza on Thursday 11 December 1997, probably oblivious to the fact that it marked almost to the month, the one hundredth anniversary of the first motion pictures to be shown in Kettering, in July 1897. The full 8-screen programme started the following day.

The extravaganza featured a premiere preview of the current James Bond 007 thriller *Tomorrow Never Dies* (1997) starring Pierce Brosnan. To add to the occasion, super model of the age, Caprice, and TV star Dani Behr, made personal appearances, supported by local talent and musicians. On the forecourt, an Aston Martin DB5 car was displayed, owned by the local developer Chris Brigstock who had loaned the car to the film's producers for an earlier Bond film *Goldeneye* (1996), and again for the latest film. Alongside the Aston martin stood a BMW motor-cruiser also used in *Tomorrow Never Dies*. The evening was a spectacular launch for the new multiplex and reminiscent of those grand cinema openings of the 1930s.

The first full programmes started briskly on the next morning and consisted of nine films spread around the eight screens. Whilst the screens showing the titles are not recorded, the films on the opening week were: *The Borrowers* (1997) starring John Goodman; *The Full Monty* (1997) starring

Robert Carlysle; *Tomorrow Never Dies* (1997) starring Pierce Brosnan; *Hercules* (1997) Disney animated feature with Kevin Sorbo as lead 'voice'; *G.I. Jane* (1997) starring Demi Moore; *Face Off* (1997) starring John Travolta and Nicholas Cage; *I Know What You Did Last Summer* (1997) starring Jennifer Love-Hewitt and Regan Phillipe; *Copland* (1997) starring Sylvester Stallone and Harvey Keitel; and *Alien-Resurrection* (1996) starring Sigourney Weaver.

Multiplex operation allows greater flexibility of programming. In this instance *The Borrowers* would be screened at times more suited to its potential audiences, as would the films with higher age group certificates. 'Block-busters' are able to be shown in different screens at the same time, thus coping with demand.

The exterior of The *Odeon* is very impressive and a welcome departure from the bland architecture of Multiplexes in general. It really looks like a cinema instead of a furniture warehouse. Readily seen when entering the Retail Park, being set on a slight rise, its two tall buttresses immediately take the eye. These buttresses support the abutment and modern architectural canopy which is 'under-lit' with spot lighting. Across this abutment is the word ODEON massively displayed in silver. The grey/blue buttresses rise above the general level of the building and are enhanced by a cubic design rising above the structure.

Behind the buttresses, the main building stretches back in a pentagonal shape. The entrance is glass fronted with three sets of double doors, above which panoramic glass panels meet the illuminated displayed sign 8 SCREEN CINEMA. Glass panels continue each side of the entrance giving a pleasant view of the inside foyer. Stone masonry continues the sidelines of the building meeting with the overall brick facia design, golden in colour, with an attractive grey/blue brick pattern running horizontally around the building. Each side of the raised entrance, ten illuminated quad poster displays are sighted for easy film information.

At night the front of the complex is lit with red and blue neon and the buttresses are floodlit in blue. The view of the decorative foyer lighting is visible through the large windows which goes further to enhance the overall external view.

Inside, the luxury that greets you is really pleasant and welcoming. The foyer is festooned with neon decorative lighting. The sales area, facing the entrance, has everything from self-service ice cream to 'pick'n'mix' confectionery. Sales points offer soft drinks and beverages, the ever-popular popcorn, and ranges of fast foods. To the right of the entrance are the admission and customer services. The tickets are issued by a computerised system, either for walk-up purchase, or by telephoned and advanced bookings. 'Queue busting' facilities are also available for patrons who have pre-booked and use credit cards for payment.

The impressive foyer. Entrance to the auditoria is to the right clearly indicated by the patterned walkway.

The foyer is tastefully decorated in shades of blue and grey with added blacks and whites. The floor is carpeted and tiled in similar colours and there is a designated 'footpath' leading patrons to the vestibule and auditoria.

The main feature of the foyer is the ceiling. Curved decorative metal frames support the illumination. Above these, there is a large circular 'dome' across which is played the word ODEON by the use of an Octo-Kinetic projector. This highly effective feature is enhanced by red and blue neon lights on the remaining area of the ceiling and other parts of the foyer. The whole presents a very attractive and unusual décor. The vestibule leading to the eight auditoria is spacious and similarly furnished. Entrance to the projection suite and administrative offices is to the rear of the booking area.

The exterior at dusk with the neon lighting of the foyer attractively visible through the glass front

The eight auditoria are in the stadium style and all decorated with dark textured walls with light grey panelling. The seats are grey/black moquette each with excellent legroom and good posture position. A drinks holder is fitted to each seat and the comfort afforded is excellent. Facilities exist for disabled patrons for which all screens are accessible either for wheelchair or the use of normal seating if preferred. The carpeting is deep-pile and predominantly grey.

Each screen has tabs in grey. Lighting is provided by decorative spot lights played on the light grey wall panels and can be selective. The seating capacities are: Screen 1, 175 seats; Screen 2, 125 seats; 3, 232; 4, 349; 5, 105; 6, 83; 7, 105; 8, 310. Thus the total seating is 1,484. In the old *Regal/Granada*, there were nearly 2,000.

In the larger screens Octo-Kinetic projectors play ODEON across the screen tabs and ceiling, as in the foyer, during any intermissions. This is highly effective and is pleasantly received, the Kettering *Odeon* Multiplex being the first of the circuit cinemas to have this experimental decoration.

Every auditorium has eight ambient speakers installed with three speakers on each sidewall and two to the rear wall. The speakers play the 'effects' tracks on the respective films.

The projection suite is well appointed and is spacious and airy. All screens are served by individual projection using the latest technology. Not all screens receive the same type of sound, the large ones have a digital system, whilst the others have analogue sound.

In all, the Multiplex is attractive, comfortable and a highly enjoyable environment, making going to the pictures a pleasure. On my visit there, the staff were pleasant and helpful, and my visit was a very enjoyable experience. A visit to the *Odeon* is as much of an occasion as going to the cinema should be, with good presentation and a feel of luxury akin to the super-cinemas of Kettering's past.

Once again, Kettering is on the map for motion-picture presentation, with a cinema which is of British design and operated by a well-known and respected British cinema circuit. Its arrival was a splendid way for Kettering to celebrate one hundred years of cinema.

Projection and technical information:

Projection:
Eight Cinemeccanica Victoria-5 projectors, one for each screen

Sound systems:
Eight Cinemeccanica CNR 3-35 complete with QSC amplifiers UIA 900 (one adjacent to each projector)
Screens 1, 3, 4, and 8 CP500 Dolby Pro-logic full THX digital sound
Screens 2, 5, 6 and 7 C445 Dolby Stereo-surround Analogue Sound

Light source:
Each projector has Cinemeccanica Zenon lamp units

Speaker set-up:
Each auditorium, Screen: rear LH-Centre-RH, high definition
Hall: ambient 8 two-way audiom

Screens:
All screens with variable masking fixed upper and lower
Aspect ratios possible between 1:66 to 1 and 2:35 to 1 available

Film feed system:
Eight Cinemeccanica mobile auto-feed three platter units (adjacent left side of each projector when operational)

Automation:
Eight Cinemation units adjacent (right) to each projector

Special Effects Lighting:
Screens 1, 3, 4 and 8 Octo-Kinetic projection.
The Kettering *Odeon* Multiplex was the first to use Octo-Kinetic projection features in the auditoria.

PART THREE

THE OTHER PICTURE SHOWS

So far I have spoken of the commercial cinemas of Kettering, but this book is concerned with motion-picture entertainment in the town, and so there is a need to describe the other venues where cinema shows took place. For some, as they read this, the memories will come flooding back, especially those who remember the shows at the Working Men's Club, which had a proper projection room and operated cinema-style. For other readers it may come as a surprise to know that films were shown in clubs in the town also in the Central Hall, alas now lost to the town, and at the ever popular Wicksteed Park. They all have a place in the cinematic history of Kettering, and therefore in the is book

THE K.I.C.S CENTRAL HALL

After 1920, when The Victoria Hall converted to a cinema, Kettering was left with no public hall. It was felt that there was a need for one but the local council was either reluctant, or unable, to build one. The Kettering Industrial Cooperative Society (K.I.C.S.) was an extremely progressive cooperative movement which had a history going right back to the Rochdale pioneers of the movement, and owned a lot of property in the centre of town particularly in the Eden Street and Saint Andrew's Street areas. In 1928 the Town Council expressed a wish to have a public hall in the town and the K.I.C.S. said that it would be willing to build the town a hall subject to the Society being permitted to hold public meetings there. With this agreed, the Central Hall was built by the K.I.C.S. Work's Department as a large public hall not only as a centre for the K.I.C.S., but fitted out as an entertainment centre for the whole town.

It was built on a strip of land stretching from Montagu Street to Eden Street, and was set back into the Arcade which ran from Montagu Street through to Newland Street. The Central Hall was opened on Saturday 19 October 1929 by the President of the K.I.C.S., Mr Thomas Adams. It was a great public occasion with the Chairmen and Councillors of the Kettering Town Council attending as did almost all of the local dignitaries. There were the usual ceremonial speeches, followed by a celebrity concert by local artistes including Carol Summers and Will Eagle.

The Hall could seat 850 downstairs and 200 in the Balcony, although later the downstairs capacity was reduced to 600 to comply with fire regulations. The stage, some 28 feet wide, was quite high and sloped towards the footlights. The front tabs were blue with gold braiding and forward of them was a safety curtain on which a pleasant scene was painted. The stage was fully equipped and full stage productions were presented in the Hall, particular those of the Kettering Operatic Society.

The Central Hall soon after opening (D. Wharton)

A projection room was built out from the rear wall of the Balcony. It was only accessible from the roof of the Arcade by an iron staircase and exterior door. The Central Hall was not used as a cinema as such, and films projected there were usually as part of a lecture, or for advertisement purposes during stage productions and exhibitions. There are few details available to be able to record any of the films shown over the years, but there are two events in which it is known that film was featured.

On Friday 9 October 1931, Amy Johnson, the famous aviatrix, gave an illustrated lecture which was entitled *How Jason and I Flew to the Land of the Golden Fleece* (Jason was the name of her Gypsy Moth biplane). The review of the lecture appeared in the *Evening Telegraph* the following evening:

> 'During the showing of the film of the scenes of her welcome in Australia, Amy sat on the raised part of the stage, perfectly at ease, and put her comment, much of it humorous. The film provided a fitting climax to a remarkable lecture the audience being roused to a high pitch of enthusiasm as they witnessed her tumultuous reception in Australia, in London and at her home.
>
> She apparently made a forced landing at Glendon the previous evening, through tiredness. Her mechanic knowing nothing of this arrived at the appointed place to prepare the aircraft for its later flight to London to be first shocked, then delighted to find Amy already at the Central Hall having a deservedly well-earned rest.'

There was at least one 'cinema-style' film presentation at the Central Hall, and that was for Thursday, Friday and Saturday 23, 24 and 25 June 1930. The film was *Palestine*, which was described as a 'realistic film'. I can find no listing for this picture and assume it was probably a religious or scientific film.

Another interesting advertisement was for the Kettering Radio Show at the Central Hall on Thursday, Friday and Saturday 24, 25 and 26 September 1936, at which all the local, and some national, radio traders would have been attending, and advertised for this event were 'free film shows'.

The Central Hall never had sound film equipment installed, and to my knowledge no sound films were ever shown unless they were on 16mm gauge. The projection equipment was removed when American troops were billeted in the Hall during the Second World War. During this time it is recorded that appalling damage was done to the hall particularly around the walls and the precious dance floor. Restoration took place after the War and the Central Hall returned to the peace time pursuits of entertainment, particularly dancing. On Saturday nights, it was a 'palais de danse' and if you wanted to see and be seen, that is where you went. Projection equipment was never installed again.

Sometime in 1978, the Leicester Co-operative Society took over the K.I.C.S. and the Central Hall closed unceremoniously. It became a warehouse and furniture shop, but thankfully is now (Summer 2000) undergoing transformation back into a nightclub.

Whilst the Central Hall was never a cinema in that sense, it did contribute to motion-picture entertainment in the town and thus deserves a mention.

Projection and technical information:

When the Hall was built 'talkies' were already becoming an established feature, and it is strange that sound equipment was not installed when motion-picture equipment was planned for the Hall. As it was, two Gaumont Chrono mute projectors were installed in a small projection room built off the back wall of the balcony and accessible only from the roof of the Arcade, with iron stairs to a steel door in the wall of the 'box'. There was one slide lantern and the usual projection room furniture. The screen was a roll-up or alternatively, the safety curtain was used.

KETTERING WORKING MEN'S CLUB

There is perhaps nothing strange in finding a cinema in a Working Men's Club. Many cinemas, particularly in mining communities, started their lives in such clubs and institutes. Working Men's Clubs were a popular and important part of this country from the 1880s onwards, and many still exist today.

Not only were they a place where the working man could go in his leisure hours, he could also take his wife and family into a far better environment than the public houses of the day. The Working Men's Clubs not only provided cheaper drinks and better services, they also provided libraries, reading rooms, educational services, outings, play areas for children, games, and many more services determined by the membership. One facet for which they were all well known, was entertainment; concerts, dancing, lunches, socials and so on, and it is not surprising therefore that some clubs also went into for cinema entertainment.

The original part of the Working Men's Club in Wellington Street, Kettering was built in 1887. Ten years later, the Concert Hall was added at the rear and consisted of a two-storey hall. The lower floor was the Billiard Room, and the Concert Room was on the upper floor, complete with a Bar, although they were separated by a large heavy wooden partition running half the length of the Hall. During shows and dances, this was opened to about six feet at the stage end to permit the passage of waiters serving drinks.

The Concert Hall was about 100 feet by 35 feet. There was a stage with a painted canvas proscenium and a dressing room either side. The front and screen tabs were of a golden colour, and the screen was fixed on the back wall. Seating capacity was about 200 and consisted of wooden chairs interspersed with round bar tables.

At a later unknown date, a small projection room was built off the rear of the Hall, and using adverts from the *Evening Telegraph* as a guide, it seems that the 'Works' (as the club was known) went into 'talkies' at Christmas time 1933. It was advertising sound films for Christmas Day morning and the evening after Boxing Day. For Christmas Day evening there was a Gala Concert, and dancing on Boxing Day evening.

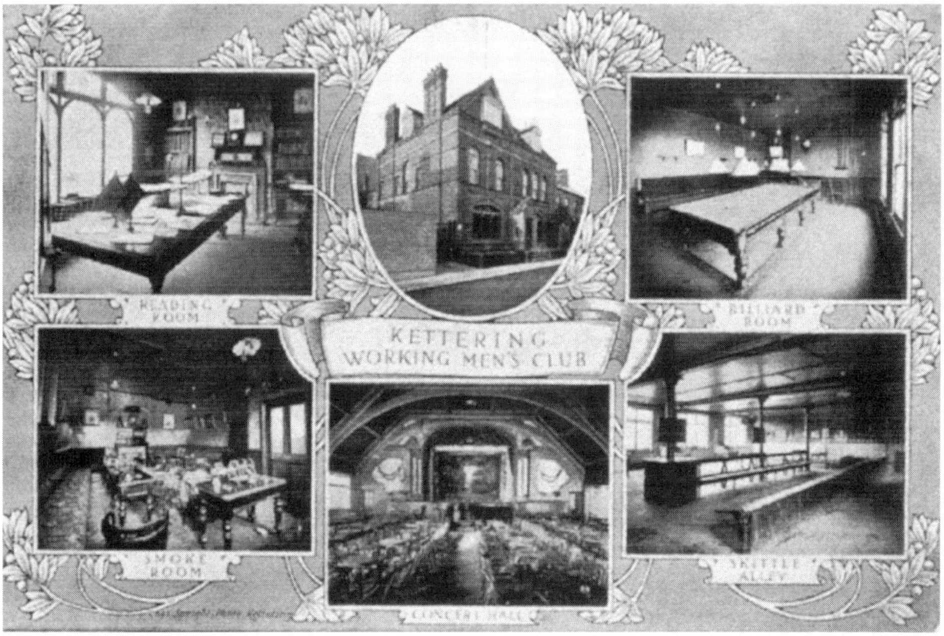

A post card showing the Concert Hall, early 1900s (D. Wharton)

Every week end from then on, films were advertised, and for many years the pattern seemed to be: for the winter months, films on Saturday nights, Sunday lunchtime and evening; and during the summer, films on Saturday, which would be 'shorts', and a feature film on Sunday lunchtimes. Previous to this, silent pictures had been shown at the club since the early 1930s, but publicity for them is obscure.

Every member and associate member could attend and full members could sign in a visitor. Prices were 3d and 4d rising later to 4d and 6d; children were half-price, and retired pensioner members got in for nothing.

The programmes for Saturday and Sunday evenings would be family films, comedies musicals and the like. The Sunday lunchtime shows were more for adults when the category 'A' and 'H' films would be shown. These Sunday shows were very popular and were the first Sunday film programmes to be shown in the town, preceding those in the main cinemas by a number of years.

For those who attended the 'Works' pictures, the place holds a host of fond memories. Sheila Mulligan remembers being taken there by her parents. She would often go to what she called the 'proper' cinemas on Saturday evenings, but she remembers the 'Works' because she was able to see her favourite films again, and this time, clutching a cream soda. She recalls that 'the films at the 'Works', although not newly released, were nevertheless good and if we had already seen them in the proper cinema they were worth seeing all over again'.

Like Sheila, I was also taken to the 'Works' by my parents. It must have been my first association with the motion picture as I could only have been about five years old. The pictures at the Club brought me in to contact with the famous people I knew from my *Film Fun* weekly comic, Arthur Askey, George Formby, Old Mother Riley, the Marx Brothers, and of course, the loveable Stan Laurel and Oliver Hardy. *Disraeli* (1929) with George Arliss is a film that, for some reason, I remember seeing there (I do not think I should have) and *Oh Mr Porter* (1937) with Will Hay, Graham Moffatt and Moore Marriott.

The film programmes would start with shorts, usually comedies or musicals, followed by a *Pathe Gazette*. After an interval, there might be another short, and then the 'big' picture. The interval was eagerly awaited because as the lights went up, through the door would appear 'Bogey' Kelsty, better known to us kids as 'the chocolate man'. He was a great character and over his arm he had a large wicker basket filled with goodies. Mine was always a Mars Bar, and even in the early part of the War despite rationing, he still seemed to have something for everyone.

I had always wanted to get up those stone steps to the projection room, but it was to be many years before I did so. The films were not resumed after the War, and with the popularity of the cinema at that time, that seems strange. In 1952 I was asked to do pilot film shows on Sunday lunchtimes to see what the response would be. At that time I was involved in 16mm mobile work and intended to show the films from the old projection room.

And, at last, after all those years, I found myself standing in the middle of the small room that still had the smell of the old nitrate film. The old 35mm projector was still there with its Vulcan arc lamp. On the side wall was the BTP amplifier rack with some of the biggest valves I have ever seen. Now I knew why we had those intervals every twenty minutes or so all those years before. There was only the one projector.

With the assistance of my father we tried to move the old projector aside to gain access for my two 16mm projectors, but it was in vain and I had to project from the floor of the Hall. But I also tried to get the old projector to work. All the electrics seemed in order, and I actually got the projector to turn over. Next the amplifier – the lamps lit and there were no bangs. But the arc lamps needed a mercury rectifier to provide the correct voltage, and alas, the rectifier shack was empty. Obviously it had succumbed to being a 'war casualty', so the possibility of any return to 35mm films at the 'Works' was doomed. So I had to show my two 16mm projectors from the floor of the Hall. A 'new' screen was created from the old screen discarded from the *Empire* which was going through its refurbishment at that time.

So for a time, Sunday lunchtime films returned to the 'Works' and very well attended they were. The programmes were *The Ghost of St. Michael's* (1941) starring Will Hay and Claude Hulbert, and supporting, was a cartoon and *The Devil Bat* (1941) with Bela Lugosi. The second programme two weeks later was *For Me and My Gal* (1942) starring Judy Garland and Gene Kelly, and the support was a cartoon and *Terror By Night* (1946) with Basil Rathbone and Alan Mowbray, a Sherlock Holmes programmer. There were many technical problems however, particularly with blackout and the need to get off the Concert Hall floor, mainly because of the 'bounce' of the floor whenever anyone passed by. Using the old projection room would have involved the Club in a lot of expense, and so after a few months the venture ceased.

In 1953 Woodleigh Mobile Cinemas, operated by Mr E. Toseland and Mr H. Sharp ran a film programme using 16mm. The film was *Maytime* (1937) with Nelson Eddy and Jeanette MacDonald, but this seems to have been the only other presentation at the 'Works'.

The Club is now a fitness centre and nothing of the old Concert Hall remains. The outer door of the old projection room can still be seen from Wellington Street, easily recognised by the steel emergency door.

Whilst not a commercial cinema as such, the 'Works' cinema has a special place in the hearts of the many who sat on hard chairs being entertained by the lovely old films it showed, and for giving us kids our movie education and for some happy and unforgettable memories.

Projection and technical information:

The late Colin Bell lists the projector installed, as being a Gaumont Chrono, and this is not disputed. However, on my visit to the projection room in 1952, the projector in situ was a Gaumont 16. This projector had an exposed shutter between the picture gate and the lens. The sound system was BTP sound head and amplification. The arc was Vulcan. The screen was on the back wall but the actual location of the speaker(s) is unknown.

Rear of the old Concert Hall. The window of the old projection room and the green emergency exit from the room are clearly visible, 1997.

Mr Toseland of Woodleigh Mobile Cinemas, informs me that when he presented his show at the Club in 1953 the projection room was clear of equipment. This indicates that the old projector and sound system were removed sometime during 1952 or 1953. Efforts to establish what happened have failed, and it can only be assumed that the equipment was destroyed. If so, this was lamentable because the projector was a valuable museum piece.

A final word about the 'Works' in that unconfirmed records show that a British Talking Pictures sound installation was fitted out in 1930. If this was so then no 'external' advertising was given for film programmes. More significantly, the installation would have been soon after the Gaumont Pavilion and certainly before the Empire and Coliseum. The equipment I found in 1952 certainly had a mute projector with sound added, but I would have, from memory and notes taken at the time, dated the BTP equipment as certainly of primitive design and possibly installed second-hand. Silent pictures could have course been shown prior to 'talkies' at the 'Works' and possibly 'talkies' before the advertising mentioned earlier, but no records exist.

MINIATURE RIFLE CLUB

RIFLE BAND CLUB

These two Clubs are dealt with together, because between 1948 and 1951 films were shown at both these Clubs on Sundays by Mr E Toseland and Mr H. Sharp of Woodleigh Mobile Cinemas. They used the same programme, showing at lunchtimes at the Miniature Rifle Club, and then showing the same programme at the Rifle Band Club in the evening.

The Miniature Rifle Club, a Working Men's Club, still survives in Hallwood Street, Kettering. The Club had no concert hall as such and films were shown in the main bar area. The projection unit of Woodleigh Mobile Cinemas was set up in the Club's Committee Room.

The film programmes were run every Sunday lunchtime between 1948 and 1951. They were very popular and many top class films were shown. One interesting inclusion in each programme was a serial, such as *Blake of Scotland Yard* (1937) with 15 episodes and starring Ralph Byrd, Joan Barclay and Herbert Rawlinson. Contrary to popular belief, there was never a projection room built, nor have 35mm films been projected at the Club.

The Rifle Band Club, off Havelock Street, also still exists and remains a Working Men's Club in the traditional sense. It is much larger than the Miniature Rifle Club and has an upper floor Concert Room where the films were shown, which could seat 200 quite comfortably. The projection unit was set up in a position to the rear of the Concert Room on a concrete slab extension. A portable screen was set up on the stage.

It is rumoured that a projection room was built, but no evidence however has been found to substantiate this, or that 35mm films were shown at the Club. Possibly the concrete slab where the Woodleigh projector was set up was intended to be the foundations of the 'box'.

As with the Miniature Rifle Club, the shows were very popular, but they had to cease in 1951 because of the increasingly high cost of hiring films.

Projection and Technical:

Woodleigh Mobile Cinemas used 16mm Carpenter projectors, which were a derivative of the American NATCO projector, and operation was from the left side. They were a very good machine and equal to the job they were put to having a very good condenser system and using a 1,000 watt incandescent lamp as the light source.

WICKSTEED PARK

The Wicksteed Park at Kettering is a very popular playground and caters for all types of leisure activities and entertainment. Laid down in 1919, it was a 'gift' to Kettering by Charles Wicksteed, manufacturer and business man, and over the years has grown into a busy amusement park with a large lake, miniature railway of some considerable prestige, boating lake, zoo, funfair and just about everything to make the children – and the adults who accompany them – happy.

It is not generally known however, that once there were cinema facilities in the Park. One of the problems with an open-air amenity is of course the weather. When it rains, what do you do? To be truthful at 'Wickies', up until 1952, the answer was not much. But this was rectified in 1952 when storage buildings in the central area of the Park opposite to the Pavilion were cleared away and a purpose-built entertainment hall was constructed which included a projection room. Named 'Coronation Hall', it still stands today.

Films were only shown during inclement weather, often that meant every day, and comprised of family entertainment with cartoons, comedies and adventure films. The Hall could seat between 300 and 400 and was equipped with tip-up seats. When films were not shown, the Hall would stage children's shows and entertainment and it was a very welcome and popular addition to the Park.

Films are not shown in the Hall now, and the 35mm equipment was disposed of some years ago. However, because of its past association with motion pictures, if only for a short time, it is worthy of mention.

Projection and technical information:

There were two 35mm projectors installed in the purpose built projection room and it is believed they were Gaumont-British 'N' type with incandescent light source. Sound reproduction was via the Hall amplification system and the speakers were situated behind the screen when films were shown. The screen was a large roll-up type positioned behind the stage proscenium.

THE TOWN BAND CLUB

Although no records have been found, it has been said that the Club was fitted out with a projection room probably prior to the 'talkies' era. Exhaustive research has failed to find any evidence to substantiate this. Old Club records were obscure, but checks through the advertisement pages of the local press reveal no publicity for films being shown at the Town Band Club.

Therefore the question of whether 35mm films, silent or 'talkie;' were shown cannot be verified and leaves me with the conclusion that films were never shown here. It is possible however, that from time to time private 16mm film performances could have taken place at the Club.

THE WINDMILL CLUB

The Windmill Working Men's Club was built on modern lines about 1935. It was spacious and on one floor with a splendid Concert Hall which was long and narrow, and broadened outwards near to the stage end which made it somewhat oddly shaped for showing pictures. Probably the only Working Men's Club with a neon sign, it was very popular.

No projection facility was ever built on to the Concert Hall but it is known, and remembered, that 16mm performances were shown from time to time around the late 1940s and early 1950s. The projection point for these shows was towards the rear of the Hall and audience. The screen was front stage and portable. It is not thought that any regular film performances ever took place at this Club.

It is possible that at the other ten Clubs in the town, pictures were shown from time to time, and for various purposes. Alas no records are available to substantiate the evidence for any performance. If there were, they would have been 16mm.

PART FOUR

TALES, MYTHS AND LEGENDS

Cinemas have created their own lore, and tales about them are legendary. They were focal points in the neighbourhood, as important as the public houses. Workers from the town's shoe factories, tanneries, engineering shops and many of the other pillars of the Kettering economy, could relieve their often drab lives by being carried into the world the cinema created for them, transported via the cinema screen. The films, the stars, the spectacle were all up there on that screen, and the very cinemas themselves became the temples where that wonder was experienced in the company of an egalitarian patronage.

Kettering cinemas were no exception to creating some of those myths. Some of the following anecdotes come from people who have strong memories of their cinema experiences, whether they worked in them or spent their leisure time there. Others have come from news reports and snippets from periodicals and some from my own memories. These yarns, and the part the cinemas played during the war years of the twentieth century, tell only part of the Kettering cinema heritage. Read them. Chuckle at them. Live with them. Each is a story in itself.

SILENT CINEMA

Kettering cinemas were *never* silent. What the films lacked in audibility the cinema itself more than made up for. The thuds as the tip-up seats went down as they were sat upon. The click of the piano reading light as it was switched on. The mechanical clatter of the projectors as they drove the film relentlessly on. The rattle of the pianist's rings and bangles as she raised the tempo to capture the pictures on the screen above. The hiss of the hygienic spray as it was carried around the auditorium spelling death to any microbes – and the customers' dandruff. The renewed clatter and bang of the tip-up seats as THE END was expected to appear, only to recede momentarily when it did not. The rustle of sweet wrappers and sucked lollipops. The occasional snore and more. Silent pictures? That, they certainly never were.

Right up until the emergence of sound in the town's cinemas, there was always some form of musical accompaniment to the images on the screen. Being a 'cinema musician', whether solo or in combination, was not always a pleasant past time. Not every picture held the attention of all the audience, and in *Vint's Electric Palace*, and the later *Hippodrome*, they could be quite noisy and uncomplimentary to the playing.

The pianist and the instrument at The *Hippodrome* were encased in a wire mesh 'cage' to protect both from the missiles pelted at them. On Fridays and Saturdays this was even more unpleasant because produce left over produce from the market outside was smuggled in and even the wire was unable to prevent the obvious. The pelting of produce was likely to have been a left-over from the earlier days of variety when, according to my grandfather, Saturday night was retribution night if through the week the acts had been considered less than the audiences expected.

It would seem that similar occurrences at The *Pavilion, Victoria Picture House* and The *Empire* were rare and perhaps that had some bearing upon the clientele. But even these houses had their share of audience participation when the projectionist got into difficulties and had a 'white screen' if the film broke or projected the wrong reel.

Common to all cinemas was the 'countdown' if by error the film's leader came up on the screen. This of course became cinema lore and can be seen even today.

The *Empire* had its own particular opportunity for audience involvement. The projection ports through the rear wall of the Balcony were only a few feet above the double seats and with the continuous performances in those days, there were moments when the film was interrupted by the heads of people moving in and out of the seats, as well as other antics. Often this was greeted by a loud chorus of 'SIT DOWN', or something more choice.

The 'raked' floor of The *Pavilion* was another noise maker. I remember in sound days, the clump of feet as people made their way to their seats or to the toilets. As I described earlier the slope towards the screen was quite steep and one tended to put feet down heavily to retain balance especially on the downward trip, so as to be able to negotiate the turn at the front. If there was more than one person, especially youngsters, it sounded like a heard of animals. Quite how it sounded in silent days without thick carpet I shudder to think.

The *Hippodrome* experimented with 'sound accompanied pictures' by placing 'actors' behind the screen who would read from scripts, shouting the words in unison with the action on the screen. Suffice it to say the films were reasonably short and the script was little more than 'help' or similar simple phrases that were important to the story.

For the actors' words to reach the audience they spoke through large sound horns. One can picture the task of watching the film to pick up the cue, reading or learning the script and having an ear for the musical accompaniment from the other side of the screen.

Quite popular too, was the introduction of 'sound effects' to action on the screen and in the case of The *Hippodrome* this ranged from chains being dragged about behind the screen to whistles and horses' hooves effects. Arthur Brogden, General Manager of *Vint's Electric Palace* was an inventive master at this, which ensured the right atmosphere for the films he showed.

The *Victoria Picture House* was above such antics, but it did have a fine orchestra, and with prestigious films, would introduce vocal interludes to specific parts of silent films. Few actual accounts have survived, but when Cecil B. DeMille's *The Ten Commandments* (1923) was shown, an augmented orchestra was enhanced by local singers, at least a soprano and tenor, who would render appropriate arias to the important scenes in the epic.

No, Kettering cinemas were *never* silent.

A 'REALISTIC' PLAY AT THE KETTERING AVENUE THEATRE

Drama did not only happen on the stage at the old *Avenue* Theatre in Russell Street. It appears that during the week of Monday 7 January 1907, the George Henry Theatre Company was performing the play *The Sledgehammer*, a play concerned with two brothers who eventually attack each other with sledgehammers, would you believe.

The play produced melodramatic excitement right enough - but not on the stage. The actors who played the brothers, Arthur Alexander Clark of Lewisham and Arthur James Murray of Walworth, took character acting a bit too far, and attacked each other in their dressing room.

Just before the final performance on the Saturday there arose a dispute about the use of hat pegs. Clothes were thrown around, followed by a violent row.

Clark attempted to strike Murray, who was the bigger of the two, and they both fell to the floor. Murray then attacked Clark with a long knife and succeeded in stabbing him in the stomach. There are conflicting reports as to what happened next, but eventually Clark was admitted to hospital – after his performance – and George Henry called the police.

Murray was arrested, and appeared at Kettering Magistrates' Court. The case was referred to the Northamptonshire Assizes, and Murray finally found star billing with a season in Bedford Prison.

TALES OF THE WHITE TIE AND TAILS

Out front or up front, the owners and managers of the cinemas were the epitome of autocracy, most ruling their *Empires, Regals* and *Odeons* with efficiency and flair. Kettering had its quota of the best, and one or two of the lesser, variety.

In the years after the Second World War there were changes particularly with the circuits and there were many comings and goings. In the early days the manager would be responsible for bookings, both films and stage, as well as ensuring the cinema was well run and presentable. The owner(s) expected good business and they required the manager to achieve their expectations. Later, with the circuit booking programmes the manager would only have some say in what was shown in his cinema. Some owners also ran the management side.

When Leo Vint opened *Vint's Electric Palace*, he put Arthur Brogden in as General Manager. Brogden was a shrewd man who wooed the new audiences to The *Electric Palace*. He was the first of the 'front of the house' men, giving the public a new experience with his variety and cinema shows.

His job was not too difficult at first because there was no opposition – in 1909 The *Avenue* was a skating rink, the Victoria Hall was still a public amenity, and The *Pavilion* had not yet been built. Brogden was an ambitious man and when *Vint's Electric Palace* was taken over by Covington in 1912, he left also, preferring to work for Leo Vint elsewhere.

By 1912 The *Avenue* had re-opened as The *Coliseum* and the manager was William Jackman. He was heralded by the press as a man of wonderful enterprise, and of course he had to be because during his time The *Pavilion* opened, and the Victoria Hall had become a picture house. He was responsible to the General Manager who was Arthur Thompson one of the owner brothers.

When The *Victoria Picture House* opened, Mr J. Needham became its manager and remained so for many years. He was rather a small man, and like all good cinema managers, was very well dressed. Always front of house to welcome his patrons, he was about keeping the image of the picture house to the fore. He was however, not very communicative and had little rapport with his staff and therefore unable to carry them along with him. He was a worrier and allowed his problems to add to his reticence. He was, for all that, still a popular manger and the public liked him.

Jack Sherwood came to Kettering from Staffordshire and married the daughter of the original owner, Frank Payne. When he took over The *Coliseum* in 1932 he established a reputation as a showman that was second to none, and became perhaps the best remembered cinema personality the town ever had.

He was a cultivated 'man-about-town' figure, slightly bent in stature, and with his sleek shiny hair, was the essence of 1930s style. He was always immaculately dressed and it was said that he looked as if he had 'stepped out of Burton's window', always striking an imposing figure as he stood in The *Coliseum* entrance.

He seemed to have an eminence about him and he was likeable, modest and rather diffident, but his shyness did not affect his drive to make The '*Col*' the leading entertainment house in the town. Apart from making changes at The *Coliseum* he was responsible for the building of The *Savoy* after the fire had destroyed The *New Coliseum*, and for a time was also owner of The *Empire*.

Mrs Sherwood was equally flamboyant. She could have been mistaken for a movie queen. Dressed in London fashions and with her white make up and heavily rouged cheeks, she would arrive at the cinema with Jack, trailing an air of elegance and near royalty. Her distinctive appearance was enhanced further by her scarlet lipstick which was so applied that she looked as if she was permanently blowing a kiss.

Harold Jackson had been the manager of The *New Coliseum* and when The *Savoy* was built to replace it, he again took the manager's post. He was well dressed and had wavy hair and always wore suede shoes. When not working on the stage preparing for shows or dealing with theatre problems, he could be found walking around Kettering with his topcoat draped around his shoulders in show-biz style. He was a likeable person always on the look out for something special and extraordinary to present of the cinema's stage.

A manager many people fondly liked was Bert Dawson. Bert started his cinema career at The *Coliseum* and was musical director for a while. When

The '*Col*' went over to pictures he went across to The *Empire* and managed that for Jack Sherwood. There he remained until the opportunity came to move higher up the ladder and he took over the management of The *Odeon* in Corby in 1940, and finally moved to The *Odeon* at Kettering in July 1942 where he remained.

Bert Dawson was a very efficient and business-like manager who was just right for the image The *Odeon* portrayed. He was always alert to the trends and his patrons' likes and dislikes.

I can remember him clearly. On Sundays during the Second World War, the doors would open at 6pm but the films were not allowed to begin until 7pm. Sixty minutes of Victor Sylvester was hard to sit through and we would 'muck about' in the Front Stalls.

One Sunday, a couple in 'our gang' got silly and we were marched into Dawson's office just by the pay-desk. I remember he read the riot act to us, took away our tickets, and told us that we were stand in the foyer where everyone could see us until a few minutes before the programme started. If we were good, he would then personally show us to our seats, if not, a month's ban. I can assure you that we were little angels for the next half-hour. The thought of no pictures for a month was punishment enough. Life was much simpler in those days.

The first manger at The *Regal* was L. Morley-Clark. He was a flamboyant character and dressed like a movie mogul with a smart double-breasted suit and a wide brimmed hat. He was even seen with the odd cigar. Not so when up front in his luxurious vestibule welcoming the patrons in what could be called 'Regal' fashion. He was much liked by his staff and patrons alike.

During the Second World War, The *Regal* Manager was Jack Goldy who originated from London but had settled in Kettering. Flamboyant he certainly was not. Staff regarded him with respect but were not over fond of him. Emmanuel (Manny) Goldy, his son, was the Assistant Manager, a job he apparently did with little relish, but had little option but to do as he was told. Apart from this, Goldy ran the cinema well enough, but had little truck with schoolboys. We would try to evade his glare as we brought our tenpenny tickets and hurried (though not too fast) down the vestibule steps. What happened to Jack Goldy is obscure, but Manny was, in 1947, the chief projectionist at The *Empire*.

There were of course many more managers in the town's cinemas, too numerous to detail here, but a few of their names are important to mention. The *Odeon* and *Gaumont* managers included Messrs Barry, Brett, Cooke and Shepherd. At The *Granada*, Messrs Palmer and Bush.

With Maurice Lee at The *Savoy* and Joseph Lee at The *Empire*, I was never quite sure whether there was any family connection between them. Maurice Lee was best remembered for his chocolate bars. In slack moments he would be found parked on a particular radiator in the foyer of The *Savoy* munching away at what ever chocolate bar had taken his fancy, only to disappear into his office if potential trouble loomed.

SCHOOL'S OUT

This report in the *Kettering Leader* during February 1930 gives food for thought for the young picture goers of this modern age.

'Headmasters in Kettering Schools are becoming concerned about the impression upon their pupils by attending the cinemas in town. Not only it seems is there a risk of learning the wrong things from what they see in the films but too much going to the pictures ids likely to affect their school work.' There followed a debate for and against in the next few issues of the paper but finally it appears to have died down and children still went to school – and the pictures.

I was too young to be one of those at that time, but I do remember managing to cram four or five visits each week as a lad, six if you counted Sunday night or the 'Works'. Between 1940 and 1943 as a Central School pupil I had to traipse from Grafton Street to the Headlands for our weekly sports and physical activity, in a line, with my fellow pupils. The trick was to ensure you were not picked to play when the teams were chosen in school (I was lousy at sport and had no difficulty in avoiding selection).

Formed in ranks, some 150 or so kids would leave after dinner-time weaving through the centre of the town to the sports field. Now on this route there were three cinemas, The *Odeon*, The *Pavilion* and The *Regal*. By the time the snake of children got to the Royal Hotel a good number of 'sports participants had left the ranks for better things.

Making sure you were in the middle portion of the 'march' you just 'dropped-out' at Wadcroft or Gas Street and hid until the coast was clear then headed for the chosen venue. The easiest was The *Regal*, slipping out of line at Gas Street and hiding until all was clear them a few pence for the ticket and a couple more pence for an 'Eldorado' and down to the front row just in time for the big picture. Thinking back, the teachers must have known what we did but most were wartime replacements and were probably pleased to 'lose' a few charges for the afternoon. I reckon even now that I learned as much from my clandestine cinema visits than I ever did at school.

GOING TO THE PICTURES

Competition for business between the town's cinemas was always hot, but it seems it was always good natured and throughout the years, there does not seem to be any serious discord between them. It is interesting to look across the years and choose some comparisons of programme.

The week The *Regal* opened at Christmas 1936, the other cinemas were putting up a strong counter. The *Gaumont Pavilion* was showing *Windbag The Sailor* (1936) with Will Hay. At The *Odeon*, Roland Young starred in *The Man Who Could Work Miracles* (1936). The *New Coliseum* was showing *Colleen* (1936) with Dick Powell and Joan Blondell; and at The *Empire* the popular star Will Fyffe in *Annie Laurie* (1935).

The Christmas programme at The *Pavilion* in 1923 was a boxing epic *The Abysmal Brute* (1923) starring heart throb Richard Denny, and *Till We Meet Again* (1923) a romantic drama. Whilst across the road The *Victoria Picture House* was showing *Peg O' My Heart* (1923) starring Laurette Taylor.

Looking back to September 1920, The *Pavilion* was showing what was described as 'a momentous sage in five parts' (reels, that is), *Riders Of The Purple Sage* (1919) from the book by Zane Grey and starring William Farnum. As a matter of interest to movie buffs, this version of *Riders of the Purple Sage* was the first of two silent films adapted from the book, the second, starring Tom Mix was made in 1925, and was also shown at The *Pavilion*. This version actually used a wide screen process and apparently was shown in that format.

At The *Hippodrome*, life as a cinema was nearing an end as it was showing *Broken Melody* (year not known) starring Martin Harvey. Little is known of this picture but a review of the time reported that the picture 'rung the very last tear from the audience'. Supporting was a Chaplin short *Charlie's Night Out* and the last episode of the serial *Lightning Raider*. Weeks later the cinema was closed.

When The *Coliseum* opened on Wednesday 12 October 1910, the Victoria Hall countered with 'High Class Varieties', which starred 'Bosanquet – The Human Violin'. For the Christmas week of 1912, *Vint's Electric Palace* was running a variety bill with 'The Bouncing Dillons' on stage and the picture *A Peep Behind The Scenes* (1912) a saga of the stage. Oddly, this (silent) picture was also shown at The *Victoria Picture House* on a split week in January 1930. At The *Coliseum* for Christmas 1912 were 'pictures on the silver screen' with *The Eighth Commandment* (1912) and *Just A Verdict* (1911).

The night that The *Empire* closed for good, the other cinemas in the town were fairing well. At The *Granada*, John Wayne was chasing Indians in 3-D in *Hondo* (1954). The *Gaumont* had Bob Hope in one of his last big-budget pictures *Casanova's Big Night* (1954). The excellent *The Wages Of Fear* (1953) starring Yves Montand was filling the seats at The *Odeon*, and the *Savoy* was screening *Jack Slade* (1953) with Mark Stevens, a Western thought exceptionally violent at the time. Those not in the cinemas or lamenting closure of The *Empire* were probably dancing to the 'Stardusters' in the Central Hall for 3s admission.

I found it fascinating to check through the programmes for the cinemas over the years, and give one final example from the cinema recession period. In the first week of 1973 The *Granada* was bumping up its audiences with a double feature of Bond pictures with *Goldfinger* 1964) and *You Only Live Twice* (1967) both starring Sean Connery. At The *Studio* there was a double bill sex show with *Language of Love* and *Do You Believe In Swedish Sin*?

In contrast, taking two consecutive weeks in May 1938 gives an example of picture going in that era:

Week beginning Monday 23 May 1938:

The *Empire*
all the week, *Roaring Timber* Richard Dix

The *Regal*
all the week, *It Can't Last Forever* Ralph Bellamy
It's All Yours Madeline Carroll and Mischa Auer
On stage: 'The Silver Sax Six'
Sunday concert: Sidney Kite and his Band

The *Pavilion*
all the week, *Angel* Marlene Dietrich and Herbert Marshall

The *Odeon*
all the week, *Riding On Air* Joe E. Brown

The *Savoy* The Opening Week
On stage 'Troise and his Mandoliers and full company
The Working Men's Club
Saturday *The Laurel and Hardy Murder Case*
Sunday Lunchtime *The Informer* Victor McLaglen
Evening Concert

Week beginning Monday 30 May 1938:
The *Empire*
Monday to Wednesday *Vengeance* Wendy Barry
Thursday to Saturday *Unknown Ranger* Frank McHugh
The *Regal*
all the week, *Heidi* Shirley Temple
Dangerously Yours Cesar Romero
The *Pavilion*
all the week, *Second Honeymoon* Tyrone Power and Loretta Young
The *Odeon*
Monday to Wednesday *Last Adventurers* Katy Walsh
Thursday to Saturday *She Asked For It* William Carson
The *Savoy*
Monday to Wednesday *Double Wedding* William Powell
Thursday to Saturday *Maytime* Jeanette MacDonald and Nelson Eddy
The Working Men's Club
Saturday Shorts
Sunday Lunchtime *Devil Horse* Noah Beery and Harry Carey
Evening *Footlight Parade* James Cagney and Joan Blondell

Add to most of these programmes a cartoon, newsreel a short and trailers, and you could enjoy well over three hours of entertainment. If The *Regal* had a stage show also, then it was four hours or so, and at the prices charged, THAT was entertainment.

PEWS IN ALL PARTS

In 1935 a Non-Conformist church was seeking ways to break into the cinema business in the town. It was planned to alter slightly the Toller Church Rooms in Meeting Lane so that film exhibition could take place there.

Church leaders from other denominations had met in December 1935 to witness a demonstration of two types of film projector prior to an order being placed. The Reverend Cornwell told those gathered that 26 million people visited the cinema every week whilst only 3 million went to church. He stated that the showing of pictures would not be in competition with the cinemas, however, there are certain pictures which are good for children to see (although nobody ever condescended to ask us, the children) and we will aim to show films which will make children feel, when coming out of OUR shows, that they have learned something.

Fears were expressed that if the churches were to show films on Sundays, that might cause the cinemas to press for Sunday opening, which prompted the Reverend Cornwell to point out that if cinemas were to show films such as the churches would show, and then took a collection, then they were welcome to open on Sundays. The proposals were to show films once every week and after the evening service. Admission would be free.

It would seem however, that the venture never took off. There were no further reports, nor were the Toller Church Rooms changed for film performances, and under 'Church Notices' in the local press there was never any reference to regular film performances. It must be assumed therefore that the proposal was not proceeded with.

TOP ROAD TOP RANK

In February 1946 there was excitement in the town at the news that a new cinema would be built as part of a large housing estate and shopping complex in Warkton Lane (known locally as the 'Top Road'). The housing estate and some shops did appear though it was many years later. And the cinema?

WORLD PREMIER KETTERING STYLE

A typical Leicester Square event took place in Gold Street on Tuesday 20 March 1951 when the World Premiere of the British film *The Browning Version* was staged, to celebrate the complete refurbishment of The *Odeon*. Michael Redgrave starred as the schoolmaster, the central figure of the Terence Rattigan novel, and Jean Kent and Nigel Patrick supported.

There were crowds in the street and The *Odeon* had been decked out with bunting as befitted the occasion. The manager, Geoff Barlow, read the many telegrams from the film industry and the highlight of the premier was a speech form the stage of 17 year old Brian Smith, a local lad, who had a leading role in the schoolboy parts.

Earlier that day, he had been to the General Hospital and the Carey Nurses' Home between which the proceeds of the premier were shared. Does anyone know what happened to Brian?

WORKING AT THE 'PICTURES'

Working in the cinema as an usher, usherette, commissionaire, projectionist or any of the other jobs necessary to run the place, was for the most part a necessity. We had to live, and that was not possible without money, not that what was paid enabled us to live the life of Riley, but it was regular work and whether full or part time there was an extra something about working at the pictures. It was the same in cinemas everywhere, and life in the Kettering cinemas was no different. The routines and tasks were, and still are, traditional, going back to the early days.

There must be reasons why people worked the unsociable hours. For some a good way of earning that little extra perhaps, for other, particularly the full-timers, it was more than earning a living. It was a 'life'. The end of the chain in the business of films. It had a certain glamour to it and an affectionate charm which, for many, has never diminished even though long past. In today's cinemas, that still exists.

Margaret McManus started at The *Regal* in August 1944 as an usherette for the princely sum of 32s per week. Her duties apart from showing people to their seats was to 'spike' the ticket halves after they had been torn, reporting the seating situations to the pay-desk and generally looking after the patrons. It sounds as if it was easy, but it was quite hard work and it did not finish until after the show, when the ashtrays had to be emptied, floors checked for fire hazards, toilets checked and sundry other duties, and then changing out of uniform before leaving the cinema. After some time as an usherette, Margaret became 'bonded' as a cashier and worked in the cinema's pay desks.

There were staff who had special jobs and she remembers Ethel Bailey who was in charge of the Circle on her shifts, and also Jean Frith who was an usherette and in charge of sales. Margaret tells that on very rare occasions the job was risky:

> 'I was once assaulted by a man who I had asked to leave the cinema. I was quite shaken. An American airman came to my aid and saw the brute off. He then asked me out and I accepted. Another time an American soldier jumped from the Circle into the Stalls landing on a woman and breaking her legs. We never did actually find out why he did it.'

Margaret eventually left The *Regal* and in 1949 started work at The *Odeon* as a cashier.

Mr and Mrs Cowan both worked at The *Savoy*. Mr Cowan started as boy apprentice electrician and his duties in the projection room were as a rewind boy. In those days as the reels came off the projectors they had to be rewound by hand for the next showing. This was a very important job and not as demeaning as the term 'rewind boy' suggests. As the film was being rewound the edges ran between finger and thumb thus checking for any damaged perforations or lifting joins. Should they be found they had to be repaired to prevent film breaks during its passage through the projector. A good projectionist started his trade this way.

Mr Cowan remembers the winter variety seasons and worked back stage with stars such as George Formby and Nat Jackley. 'One week we had Jane of the *Daily Mirror* booked on stage but the comic strip was more exciting'. London producer Derek Salberg was responsible for most of the stage productions. Top stars stayed at the *Avenue Hotel* just up the street but the lesser artists were put up with Mrs Baker who ran a boarding house for theatricals in Waverley Road. She was the mother of the famous musician Kenny Baker.

Mrs Cowan worked as an usherette at The *Savoy* in the 1950s and her hours were from 6pm until 10.30pm for which she earned £2 per week. Duties were much the same as Margaret MacManus', and very hard on the feet.

Mr David Allan remembers his time as a projectionist at The *Odeon* when the manager was Mr Cooke. The projection room was very modern and had 'projectormatic' which was a 'robot' and the whole performance was programmed on to this machine which contained a perforated drum into pegs were inserted to match the times and functions of opening curtains, operating lights and starting the projectors. It was frowned upon by projectionists because it was automating the job. David remembers one important function which had to take place on time every day at The *Odeon*:

> 'The *Gaumont* shared its newsreel with The *Odeon* and to ensure that it was screened before the main feature at The *Gaumont* we had to have it shown by 6pm, off the projector and rewound and then any available projectionists, usually the rewind boy or the third, raced down Bakehouse Hill, hail, rain or shine with the reel and into the side door of The *Gaumont*, up those winding stairs to the projection room for threading onto their projectors. There were some pretty tight situations I can tell you. The reel then had to be returned for our last showing about 8.45pm when it was The *Gaumont's* turn to panic.'

The Chief projectionist at The *Gaumont* was Archie Mason. He started at the cinema in 1915, when it was The *Kettering Electric Pavilion* as a chocolate boy earning 7s a week. After his release from the army in 1919 he returned to the cinema working as an usher. Over the years he graduated to the job that he most enjoyed, showing the pictures, and when The *Gaumont* closed in 1959 he continued for a while at The *Odeons* in Kettering and Corby. His wife Florence also worked at The *Gaumont* as a cashier, but she was the first violinist in the pit orchestra at The *Victoria Picture House* when they had first met.

Archie was one of the band of respected chief projectionists in the town who had spent much of their working lives at the same cinema. Archie was again in the news when in 1998 a personal short reel of film that he had bought many years earlier of the RMS *Titanic* disaster, was discovered by his wife and was featured in the press and TV in the wake of the much acclaimed movie *Titanic* (1997).

Another chief projectionist was Lance Roberts who was the chief at The *Odeon*, and I believe at The *Victoria Picture House*, for many years. In my time as a projectionist I heard many stories about Lance and the way he ran The *Odeon* projection room. This is an example. Near to every projection room there was the essential fire-fighting equipment, which in those days would be fire buckets, some filled with water and some with sand (though I hasten to add NOT for projector fires). The story goes that Lance insisted on having the water in the buckets changed daily and the sand 'combed', and the outsides of the buckets had to be polished to a brilliant sheen. I visited The *Odeon* projection room often, and I can remember the place being spotless and shining like a new pin. Dirt and dust of course were, and are, deadly enemies of films and projectors.

Another chief projectionist I must mention is Eric Walters of The *Regal*. Eric came to Kettering from London, after having started at the old *Stoll Theatre* in London, becoming a projectionist in the days of silent films and seeing the advent of the 'talkies', as of course, many had. I understand he was at The *Regal* at its opening and remained throughout to The *Granada* days, though whether this was until the closure I know not. Eric was quite a character and ran his projection room in a quiet and efficient manner. You always knew when he was around because you caught a whiff of his pipe (even when it was not alight). He was a good chief to work for and a cinema character.

Life as a projectionist for most, including myself, was a way of earning a living, though as I remember, the living was pretty mean. I cannot speak for others, but I just loved my job, and still do. I was once told by Eric Walters that as he saw it hundreds of people had worked together to produce the films we showed, and it was up to us to 'put the icing on the cake' even though sometimes the cake was pretty sad.

Saturday was the busy day. In the projection room soon after 8am the first job was cleaning down the floors and projectors. This was done in time for the Saturday children's show. The 'Granadiers' were already queuing in the alley below, noisy little tykes, giving us a preview of what was to come. On screen by 9.30am with shorts or a comedy which was followed by *Uncle Jack* with fun and games, and not forgetting the birthdays.

After the ice cream stampeded it was down to serious business with Hopalong Cassidy, or another Saturday morning favourite, scuppering the villains, to the delight of the young audience. Relative silence then followed as the eagerly awaited next episode of the serial was played out, and as 'at this theatre next week' came on the screen, exit doors crashed open and a rush to beat the playing of the National Anthem took place. Why we bothered to show the trailer I was never sure because even by the end of the short version the Stalls were empty save for a few hangers-on.

The Saturday morning features were often the old inflammable nitrate film stock. Like all projectionists I had a fire now and again and seeing the black and white picture suddenly begin to transform into a sepia-toned one was no joke, especially when the little people down there knew what was happening. Thankfully the extinguishing systems on the projectors were very efficient.

The rest of the day was just as busy. Being Saturday it would be nearly full houses all day with continuous performances starting about 1.30pm. In those days, the programme, whether a split week or six-day, changed on Saturdays, and the films for next week, and often the separate one for Sunday, would arrive by 5pm or so in the evening. As the last complete performance came off the screen, it had to be 'plated-off' from the running spools and packed away in its cans and transit case and humped down to floor level for picking up by Film Transport (this is where I got long arms and all the muscles).

As the main feature came off from the last run all but the final reel would be plated off and the transit case taken down, less the final can, which we took down as we went home. I remember one Saturday, Film Transport came earlier for some reason, and finding the transport box for the feature open ready to receive the last reel, the driver closed it and was off on his way. Some quick thinking caught him at Bedford and he had to come all the way back for it. As I remember he was not too impressed.

Charge at Feather River was one of a number of 3-D films we showed. With 3-D, one needed to wear special Polaroid spectacles. These were issued to patrons as they paid for their tickets and handed in when leaving. I remember one afternoon during that week returning to the projection room via the Circle (something we occasionally did to check the projection standards) and noticed an elderly lady sitting in the upper tier of seats intently, or so it seemed, watching the picture without having the special glasses on. At first I thought she may have been asleep but as I watched, she was obviously intent on the screen. I quietly asked her why she was not wearing the spectacles, as she could not possibly see the picture without them. She looked at me and said 'Thank you young man for your concern, but I am able to see quite well without glasses'. I pointed out that the picture is fuzzy without the special glasses, 'Oh those, I gave those to the usherette and told her that I have my own spectacles thank you. As for the picture I can see it quite clearly and it's very exciting isn't it?'

Incidentally, talking of 3-D, the first Warner Brothers film in NaturalVision was *House of Wax*, but the director Andre de Toth could not see his finished product. He was blind in one eye.

STANDING ROOM ONLY

How many times all those years ago did we hear that call as we stood in the queue in Wadcroft, Gold Street, Meadow Road or outside the cinemas? What of the people who shouted 'one double at two and nine' or 'standing room only', the Commissionaires. They were cinema characters in their own right, with seemingly, as much authority as the managers themselves – and occasionally – more.

There was Mr Turner out on those marble steps of The *Electric Pavilion* and later the plain surroundings of The *Victoria Picture House*. He was an ex military man (as many were) and he gave out an air of authority around the front of the house which no one was prepared to challenge. His reputation was said to be such that no one, but no one, got past him without his knowing.

At The *Coliseum* was Harry Ball, the children's favourite. It was often said that he was more famous than the stars who trod the boards in the theatre. Children, if they were good, were often treated to a visit to his home nearby to see the parrot that he kept and the feathered attraction became equally as famous locally.

The *Regal* had 'Pop'. There was really no other like him. He was very strict with the youngsters, and like Turner, one had to get up very early to pull a trick on him. I remember him as being a fair man and if he thought you were a 'good un' he would let you in on an afternoon to see a Warner Brothers gangster film, usually an 'A' certificate, but woe betide you if you were foolish enough to mess about once inside. In later years Harold Carpenter wore the braid and carried on the tradition but his time was the saddest – he saw the closure of the cinema. Those loveable characters, the bane of enterprising schoolboys, but respected by everyone, have now all disappeared. The 'power' they wielded would be totally incomprehensible to today's youth, brought up as they are, to question and dispute any form of authority.

BOYS WILL BE BOYS

In my research I received a number of written memoirs from people who had fond memories of their cinema going days. One such contributor was Alah Buksh who provided many anecdotes. He writes of Mrs MacManus, who, he admits, on one or two occasions, was asked by her to leave The *Regal*. He says 'this would be so if they were showing a Nelson Eddy and Jeanette MacDonald picture whereupon we lads would be on our worst behaviour, whereas, if it was dear old Humphrey Bogart up there on that screen we were always on our best behaviour. Of course, if we had no money, we came in through the back exit door in Meadow Road.'

This was a favourite trick at The *Regal*. Money would be pooled and then a couple of lads would pay. The Men's toilet was by those exit doors and at an appropriate time, one of the 'payers' would conveniently go to the toilet and let the others in the toilet where they would all congregate before coming out in dribs and drabs. The penalty for being caught was a ban.

Alah writes 'The *Empire* was renowned for its double seats at the rear of the Balcony. Some of these had their view interrupted by supporting columns but the occupants were not all that bothered. The *Odeon* was a bit more up-market, with its smart foyer and curving stairway up to the Circle. The cinema had a 'four-square rigged' commissionaire with whom many a Kettering boy worth his salt had at least one run-in.'

COLD COMFORT

The years following the Second World War were very austere indeed and the early part of 1947 was particularly uncomfortable. Severe weather conditions had laid the country under many feet of snow and thick ice during February and March. The arctic climate seriously affected just about everything including fuel and food and in less than two years after the finish of the War, the populace found themselves back to severe rationing, and restrictions on the use of electricity were acute.

The world of entertainment was seriously affected, sport was cancelled, and the cinemas severely affected. The government of the day brought in measures to contain the emergency, and Kettering's cinemas were required to do their part in helping fuel conservation. Afternoon shows were abandoned and the evening shows were curtailed at 10pm, returning them to hours experienced during the early bleak years of the war. Even the Saturday morning children's shows had to be cancelled for one month to meet the requirements.

The crisis that began in February lasted until mid-March, and only then were the cinemas able to revert to normal opening times. Even during the first years of the War the curtailment of opening was not as severe as that experienced during the dreadful winter of 1947.

WHEN THE ELK RIDES IN FOR THE BIG POW-WOW

March 1926 saw a publicity stunt in Kettering that was to stir the hearts of every 'brave' in the reservation. The *Empire* was showing the Western pot-boiler *The Thundering Herd* (1925 Paramount) starring Jack Holt, Noah Beery and a real Indian Chief 'White Elk'. This picture was what Westerns were all about. Indian raids, cattle drives across the prairie, guns spitting, arrows flying. Just the stuff for The *Empire* audiences.

To publicise the film, Paramount despatched the great Indian chief to England to rustle up the local tribes to make sure they attended the big pow-wow in the cinema tepees. Travelling north, he rode into Kettering and tethered his stallion (actually it was a mare from a local horse owner) to the hitching rail outside The *Empire*. He then proceeded to the flat roof of the shop on the corner (the local saloon, the *Swan*, was serving hostile ranchers at the time) and performed his tribal dance to the accompaniment of his own hoots and yells. It is reported that the local sheriff, complete with helmet and size tens, managed to keep the peace.

THE GIRL UPSTAIRS

Miss Elsie Pearson set somewhat of a precedence when on Wednesday 28 January 1942 she took over the role as the chief projectionist at The *Savoy*. Daughter of the chief maintenance engineer for the K.I.C.S. Central Hall, Elsie started work in the cinema business at The *Empire* when she left school. She worked her way up to second operator there, and when the opportunity arose, she applied for, and got, the chief's job at the bigger theatre.

There were many instances during the War where female projectionists took over in the cinemas of Britain when the men were called up, and some became chief projectionists. The *Savoy* can lay claim to one.

HERE COMES CHARLIE?

If it was Chaplin you wanted to see then The *Pavilion* was nearly always the cinema where you would find him. All of his great films showed there right up until the installation of sound and beyond. Chaplin, as is well known, shunned the new 'talkies' except for music and effects, and continued with his silent pictures for many more years.

One such film made around the advent of sound was *The Circus* (1928) telling the story of a man on the run from the police taking refuge in a circus. For this picture he got a special Academy Award for versatility as an actor and director. The film showed at the *Pavilion* shortly before the cinema was wired up.

The mention of Chaplin leads to a controversy that has raised its head on more than one occasion. Did Charles Chaplin once come to Kettering to publicise a film? There are conflicting reports. Two articles from the local press in the late 1970s, make some interesting speculation.

The first article talks about a house in Wadcroft, number 30, owned by Mrs Susannah Hawthorne, at which Chaplin stayed for two weeks whilst making personal appearances to publicise the showing of his *The Escaped Convict*. It gives no date, but describes the film as 'one of his earlier screen efforts' and talks of the days when he was an 'almost unknown film player'. The article goes on to say that there was not too much room in the house in Wadcroft and he had to sleep with Mrs Hawthorne's two sons in a big iron bed.

To advertise the picture he would walk around Kettering dressed in a convicts garb and shoes on the wrong feet. Children would wait for hours outside of 30 Wadcroft for him to appear, and then follow him around town.

The second article quotes a letter disputing the first article, and was reproduced as a feature in the paper. The letter implies that it was not Chaplin in Kettering, but a look-a-like employed by the cinema to promote the film. Another writer quoted in this feature supported the original article by saying that he actually talked to Chaplin and was convinced of his authenticity because of the dress and the fact that his accent was perfect. However, this writer mentions the date as about 1926 and the film *The Prisoner*.

Was it, or wasn't it Chaplin? It is difficult to say without more evidence forthcoming. Research however puts both viewpoints in some doubt. Unless there are film titles still unknown, Chaplin never made a film called *The Escaped Convict* nor *The Prisoner*. The only film with which there could be any similarity was *The Pilgrim* (1923) telling the story of an escaped convict who is mistaken for a clergyman and goes about doing good deeds with hilarious results. The film was said to have more sentiment than laughter.

Another doubt is that if the film was *The Pilgrim*, then that would be shown at The *Pavilion* about 1924, nearer the time of the second article's date. But at that time, it is a known fact, that Chaplin was in America directing *A Woman Of Paris* (1923) for United Artists which starred Adolphe Menjou, and then went straight on to make *The Gold Rush* (1924) which took the best part of a year to complete. With that workload it would seem that a visit to England to promote a 38 minute film, even though it had some importance as a 'work' would have been most unlikely, especially for two whole weeks.

As for the first article, probably some promotion may have taken place, when Chaplin was 'an almost unknown film player' who may have made some short films with the Fred Karno's troupe prior to their first American tour of 1910. Chaplin's first recorded film is *Making A Living*, made in 1914 during Fred Karno's second visit to America, when Mack Sennett had spotted the potential of the young Chaplin.

So the truth about whether or not Charlie Chaplin visited Kettering may never be known. But I for one would not want to deprive the writer of that letter in the second article his treasured memory, for, as we all know, anything is possible in the world of the cinema.

HAIL...HAIL ROCK AND ROLL

Talk to anyone about The *Granada* and the conversation will very quickly turn to those glorious one night stands during the 1950s and 1960s. In association with music impresarios and recording companies Granada Theatres operated what were probably the earliest tours by pop stars in the country. Twenty-one shows in twenty-one days, touring *Granada* cinemas from Tooting to Grantham and Kettering to Shrewsbury. They came around about every six weeks or so, each a star packed show.

The pop stars are too numerous to mention, but included Cliff Richard, Tommy Steele, Billy Fury, Brian Poole and The Tremolos, Gene Vincent and some of the earlier groups such as Johnny Kidd and The Pirates. Then there was Helen Shapiro, Manfred Mann, Cilla Black, Winifred Atwell, The Searchers, Marty Wilde, Lonnie Donnegan, and Adam Faith. Not the Fab Four however, the nearest the Beatles ever got to Kettering was an appearance at Northampton.

There were full supporting 'acts' some of whom were to make the big time later. What were these shows like? I count myself as being privileged to have worked back stage on some of them and I cannot recall experiencing anything like them

The house was always sold out. The first show was about 6.30pm and lasted two hours with a short interval. There was a second show about 9pm or later. The screams started even before the show began and when it did the noise was deafening, not from the bands on stage, although they were pushing up the decibels, but from the audience.

The first half would start with an up and coming act or band and end with one of the big names. The second half would open with another rising recording star and end with another big name. There could be as many as three big names in one show, such was their quality.

Older people were not forgotten either. 'Quieter shows' with Max Bygraves, Mark Wynter, Joe Brown and The Bruvvers, Susan Maugham, Rolf Harris and other top stars of the day. The Max Bygraves show, as many did, overran to the point where he was still on stage well past midnight.

Everyone 'mucked in' on those shows even the stars. I saw Billy Fury and Emile Foord (*What Do You Want To Make Those Eyes At Me For?*) sweeping the stage before a show. Above the audience in the Stalls, were 'flown' huge loudspeakers to throw the sound to those in the Circle.

When Cliff Richard appeared, the High Street was completely blocked with teenagers, and adults, just waiting in the hope that they may catch a glimpse of him as he entered. They were to be rewarded for their long wait, but once inside Cliff was virtually a prisoner until the early hours when to escape the crowds still milling about all the exits, he was smuggled out and to his hotel. It was the same when the Rolling Stones appeared. You just could not get in or out of the cinema and the High Street was amass of people.

The atmosphere of these shows bears only one description –'wonderful'. They were noisy, wild and relentless but never problematic. Kettering had seen nothing of the sort before and has not since, and all for 3s, 5s or the front seats for 7s 6d and 10s. Rock and Roll had come to town and stage shows were back on the old *Regal* stage, in the old *Regal* tradition.

BAND CALL

Would you ever expect to hear a bugle band playing in an operetta? Well it did happen way back in November 1960 at The *Savoy*. The Kettering and District Theatrical Society staged *White Horse Inn*, their annual show, at the theatre and the producer decided he wanted a spectacular welcome to the Emperor Franz-Josef in one particular scene. Having no military band available the task was given to the Kettering Sea Cadets drum and bugle band (best in the district – I know, I was an Officer in the unit at the time).

The boys, on cue, were to strike up in the foyer, split into two columns, march down each aisle of the auditorium and on to the stage from each side, then counter-marching onstage whilst heralding the Emperor with a fanfare. The performance was for six evenings and a matinee and I remember the audiences in the Stalls being lifted out of their seats when the band struck up behind them in the foyer.

It was a spectacular scene and the boys received a standing ovation from the audience on the last night. A large cake, shaped like a ship, made by my wife, was presented to them which I can say was completely demolished within a few minutes after reaching the dressing rooms. Quite what Benatzky and Stoltz would have made of it is open to question.

ROLLING OUT THE BARREL ORGAN

Cinema managers were always out to publicise their cinemas and the films showing. One that comes to mind at The *Granada* was when the film *April Love* (1956) starring the singing heart throb of the time, Pat Boone, was shown, in, you guessed it, April. The story, filmed in Cinemascope and aimed at teenagers, concerned a young man who was sent to his uncle's farm to work out a probation order. It was a re-make of *Home in Indiana* (1954) starring June Haver.

On the Saturday the small number of cinema staff that could be sparred for a few hours, myself included, were told to bring jeans and check shirts, if we had them, and be ready to go on the street after the finish of the children's show.

At that time Kettering Round Table had acquired a barrel organ of some importance and when we mustered in the alley by the side of the theatre, lo and behold, there was the manager waiting with this rather large instrument at his side. Suitably fixed with cut outs of Pat Boone and Shirley Jones, with the film's full title on display, we began a five hour tour of the shops playing the organ and collecting for local charity.

I do not know how much we collected, or who benefited, but I do remember that the organ was very difficult to push and that handle work was hard work because once a tune was started you had to keep turning until it was finished. The only thing we did not have was a monkey. No one volunteered for the job.

It was good fun and one of the enjoyable benefits of working in the business. I do remember however, that on our last trek down Market Street to get back to the cinema, all of us pretty tired, we lost control of the Barrel Organ and it began to run away, as everybody hung on for dear life, as I (my last turn at the handle) had to run alongside still playing *For Me And My Gal* in just a little faster tempo than normal. Not being able to turn the instrument a sharp right to enter the High Street without serious mishap we ended up in the entrance to the Royal Hotel much to the amusement of bystanders and the amazement of hotel residents.

These have just been a few snippets about some of the life and times of Kettering cinemas through the ages. There must be many more, which go to make up a social history and to show how important the cinemas were in the town and in our lives. I feel that I have barely scraped the surface of the historical wealth that lies still undiscovered about our old cinemas and their characters. However, I think the following deserves a section on its own

THE WAR YEARS

The importance of the cinema during the years of the Second World War have been well documented, outlining its roll in the entertainment necessary for morale of both civilians and forces. Never before, or since for that matter, was an entertainment industry marshalled with such energy and proliferation to provide enjoyment and information to the masses, and of course it was the film industry that was enlisted to capture for all time the horrors and suffering, as well as the victories of those days. We must not forget also the wonderful films that came out of the War years both from Hollywood and Britain. Those of us who can remember them each have our favourites which carry with them the memories of those dark days.

What of life of Kettering cinemagoers during those years? Before dealing with the Second World War, just a brief glimpse into the cinema of the Great War. Cinema was less than twenty years old, as we know it, and had gained momentum as a popular entertainment. During the Great War years some wonderful films were to come from the new Hollywood, itself only a few years old. D. W. Griffith's *Birth of a Nation* (1915) and *Intolerance* (1916) to name just two. Both were shown at The *Electric Pavilion.*

For the first time though, audiences were caught up in the tragedy of War, for regularly on the screen, reports and newsreels of the conflict were shown whereby the deaths of our forces were there for all to see. Little wonder that the medium of film was also used for propaganda.

Looking at the first Christmas of the War, The *Electric Pavilion* was showing a rousing programme guaranteed to lift the heart and mind. *The Call* (1914) starring the Vitagraph star Clara Kimbell-Young was topping the bill and supported by what was possibly the first adaptation for the screen of

Charles Dickens' *A Christmas Carol* (1914) starring another top Vitagraph actor, Earl Holliman in the role of Scrooge.

The following week starting on Boxing Day 1914, the cinema was showing *Under Two Flags* (1914) with Alan Hale (yes, the same Allan Hale who starred with Errol Flynn years later). The film was a three reeler and one of the last produced by the struggling Biograph Company. The audiences loved these potboilers and the cinema was crowded at every performance over the Christmas season.

As for The *Palace*, formerly *Vint's Electric Palace*, they had variety and pictures showing the latest news from the front during that week.

What must have been the gloomiest Sunday of the century, 3 September 1939 saw the announcement declaring War and in the communiqué following, a list of the many things we took for granted and held dear, came to a stop. One of these was going to the pictures.

If what had happened in other countries so far was to happen in Britain, then within hours the cities and towns would be under attack by air-raids, and the government, rightly, did not want high civilian casualty figures caused by the bombing of cinemas, theatres, dance halls, football stadia and such like, so it closed them all. As the days passed however, and such threats were not imminent (the 'phoney war') the government realising the need and importance entertainment would have for the populace, reviewed the situation and permitted entertainment to re-open.

Cinemas across the country were open within hours. For theatres it was more difficult as actors who were reservists were called-up, and the shows folded. Other entertainment was similarly affected.

Kettering cinemas were duly closed on Monday 4 September. An announcement in the special *Evening Telegraph* issued on Sunday 3 September stated that cinemas and other places of entertainment were to close immediately as a measure of safety.

For a whole week the halls remained dark and closed, until the relaxation, and on Monday 11 September they re-opened, but with imposed operation times, which meant they opened in the early afternoon and continued to 10pm. This pattern was to continue for most of the War years.

Kettering was considered a 'safe' area and because of it saw its population grow considerably. First came the evacuees from the London area and south coast. Later the town became a near garrison with hundreds of servicemen stationed nearby and in accommodation in the town. Then came the Americans and finally prisoners of war. The town was bursting at the seams.

The cinemas were the main entertainment other than dancing at the Central Hall and George Hotel. When you consider that within easy reach of Kettering were the airfields at Desborough, Harrington, Grafton Underwood, and farther afield at Benefield, camps at Wicksteed Park and other open spaces around the town and in halls within the town. There was a massive injection of people into Kettering and district. The cinemas had never experienced such a vast potential audience as this and rose to the occasion.

After the re-opening, no longer were the bright decorative neon lighting of The *Savoy* and The *Regal* able to coax us inside, and along with The *Odeon* saw their lights diminished by the blackout restrictions. In the beginning one hardly knew they were open, for no lights were permitted outside, or shining out, but once inside there was no doubt it was business as usual.

The threats or thoughts of air raids did not seem to deter picture-goers and ample warnings of the sounding of the sirens were displayed. The cinemas showed slides and provided advise. Not to have the show interrupted The *Regal* had a large display which read AIR RAID WARNING/ALL CLEAR by the side of the stage. The cinemas carried on.

It was still possible to have an ice cream. It was lacking in quality but cold. Sweets could be had by using your coupons but generally sales were limited. I can recollect, along with my mates, taking raw carrots (suitably scrubbed) to the pictures to eat. Windows taped across to prevent flying glass in the event off bombing, queuing in the pitch dark the Commissionaire looming out of the darkness to report seat arrangement and after the show, into the darkness once again to catch the few buses homewards with the dim slits of light of their headlamps making them barely visible.

Very soon there was a movement to open cinemas on Sundays. This had been mooted in the years immediately before the outbreak of War but had not met with success because of strong opposition from the religious bodies in the town. The need was at its greatest now and with the National Emergency holding sway the objections were swept aside and cinemas were permitted to open to show films on Sunday evenings, provided they did not start before 7pm. This was to preserve the evening worship hours and conveniently arranged so that people could go to church first then to the pictures if they so desired.

If you wanted to go into any cinema at all on a Sunday night you had to be queuing at 5pm. Doors opened at 6pm to get people off the streets. This situation was to remain until 1947 when there was a move to rescind the Sunday opening as 'hostilities had ceased and a return to peacetime practices

This 1939 advert shows how entertainment in Kettering was coping with the first few months of the Second World War. Note the special offer. Betty Driver, of course, is known to us today as the barmaid Betty Turpin/ Williams of Coronation Street (Evening Telegraph)

was desired'. All the old chestnuts were roasted again but the cinemas successfully retained their Sunday opening and in fact the hours were increased. It always seemed strange to me that whilst you could not show pictures on Sundays you could have celebrity concerts and the like.

Kettering was to benefit from the closure of many London theatres for the duration. Top stage acts came to the town, and from all accounts they loved to perform on Kettering stages. The *Savoy* was the foremost in stage presentations, regularly booking radio stars, and its first big stage show after the declaration of War was *Carry On Kettering* with a host of top-liners from the London West End. The Sunday before the opening, the show advert read 'Len Young, the BBC "Singing Fool", Hear him on the air Saturday night-see him at the Savoy Sunday night.'

The *Regal* was not left behind. It was still presenting top-line concerts right through the War years. An example of the quality can be seen with the advert for Sunday 28 January 1940 when Sandy Powell appeared with a full supporting company. The following Sunday, 4 February, Harry Roy presented a new musical production *Youth In Rhythm*. Seats were priced from 6d.

The *Regal* also presented some full week bookings such as for the week Monday 11 November 1940 when a show called *Music Spectacular* with 20 supporting musical acts were presented. The cinemas were now a priority for film releases and some top films were being shown in Kettering at the same time, and sometimes before, the London release.

The wartime record for Kettering was second to none. In addition to entertain the masses they were in the forefront in helping the war effort. In January 1940 the management of The *Savoy* was announcing help for the Kettering Poor Children and the Evacuees Wartime Clothing Fund by arranging collections during performances all the week.

Over at The *Regal* the management was helping the Kettering Half-penny Shoe Fund by arranging collections every Friday night for a season. Collections for other causes were commonplace at all cinemas and when the special war effort weeks came around the cinemas were miniature exhibition halls with a multitude of service equipment on display for *Warship Week* and *Spitfire Week* and other war effort events.

I remember being involved in similar collections a year or so later when as a sea cadet I helped collect for a number of charities in cinemas. One that stands out was a collection during a week run of two naval films that had return bookings to The *Regal*. A double feature programme it comprised of the famous *In Which We Serve* (1942) and *Lady Hamilton* (1941). Collections were being taken that week for the Doctor Barnados associated *Arethusa* Training ship, which looked after boys (some of which were wayward).

A gentleman of some years would come annually to make this collection which would be preceded by himself singing a couple of songs, accompanied by a pianist, one of which I remember as *A Bachelor Gay Am I* (you would not get away with that these days, with the silly direction our language has taken) to a somewhat luke warm applause. I am sure that one way to get him off quickly by the audience was to get the collection boxes filled. For the Sea Cadets however they got to see the pictures free, so we were there every night.

For me as a lad the wartime picture going perhaps holds the greatest memories. I remember the Sundays especially. By 5.30pm we were in the queue for the pictures and this was an education in itself. The *Regal* queue started in the High Street and stretched down Gas Street (Meadow Road). The *Pavilion* queue was contained in the Wadcroft and it would sometimes wind around that semi-circular street until the end was visible by Woolworths. The *Odeon* was the best queue. It began in what was then the Post Office Arcade and stretched right back to the Legion Club and beyond. If it was a wet evening you had to get there early to get underneath the front of the arcade which was covered. Talk about social education. You met everyone there and I cannot remember there ever being any trouble.

Anything up to an hour later you got into the cinema. The earlier you got in the longer was the wait for the 7pm start. It was noisy but good-humoured and any bad behaviour was quickly stamped upon. We liked The *Regal* best for the long wait and would get in the queue early because once inside they were playing all the latest music. Not so at The *Odeon*. There it was dear old Victor Sylvester and his Ballroom Orchestra, on record of course. The '*Pav*'. was playing selections from the musical shows. Then at 7pm sharp the lights went down and if your date had shown up (usually inside the cinema) you got settled down, if not, well you had probably seen it anyway, as Sunday films were always re-runs and separate programmes from the week.

Alah Buksh relates how he was one of the 'nicer' boys and occasionally was shown the door:

> 'One of these occasions was in 1944 and at a time of severe shortages in Britain. It was Sunday night at The *Odeon* and a large group of us schoolboys occupied the front rows. One of the lads

> had a banana, which his airman brother had brought back from doing his bit in North Africa. Bananas of course were totally absent from our lives and dozens of us were frantically climbing over seats to have a look at this strange thing. Needless to say we were shown the door and banned again for another week or two.'

I mentioned earlier that being in the cinema queues was an education. I think we learned more about human nature and peoples of the world there than we ever did at school. Not only would you stand with your own friends and other towns-people but there were Service personnel, some of whom could really spin a yarn.

Americans, some of them black and we had never seen any black people except on the screen, gave us gum and told the darnd'st tales. I remember once waiting in the queue for The *Pavilion* and quite near to us there were three or four black soldiers. We struck up a conversation with them but this was cut short by two tall white Americans (we took them to be Army police) who hoisted them out of the queue telling them to wait until all the people in the queue had entered the cinema. I can remember we were quite upset and could not understand it.

There were also German and Italian prisoners of war, whose camps were nearby, who could come into town. I cannot remember how we felt about them and quite what they made of us, I cannot say, but we could not understand why they left the cinema before the end, until we found out they had a curfew. It is interesting to note that we never felt scared about any of these experiences.

As the War progressed and I grew up I learned about the great conflict from the newsreels we saw at the cinemas. No Errol Flyns or John Waynes here but the real thing. We did not read the newspapers (only to see what was on at the pictures) but the good old *Gaumont-British, Movietone* and *Pathe News* kept us up with the war.

There were of course the countless films about the war that we saw, and thinking back it was always the British films that impressed us most. *In Which We Serve, The Way Ahead, We Dive At Dawn, Went The Day Well* and so forth, though anything with Humphrey Bogart or James Cagney and the like were equally acceptable, and for me especially, those wartime musicals with al the big names bands of the day, Goodman, James, Miller, and not forgetting Betty Grable, Alice Faye, Bette Davis …ah, those memories.

Looking back I realise that young people like myself were shielded to some degree from the horror that was taking place world wide, and that living in Kettering we were reasonably safe from the bombs and blitzkriegs elsewhere. For some there was a realisation of this, when inevitable losses of family and friends occurred, and so their youthful lives were blighted by those experiences. But for many young people it was a bit of an adventure in some ways. The cinemas took away the bleakness of the war years and although Kettering might not have been in the very thick of the struggle, its cinemas can be proud of the effort they made to keep us entertained and our spirits high.

PART FIVE

'THE LITTLE GEMS'

This book is about the cinemas of Kettering, and in the present day, the towns of Rothwell, Desborough and Burton Latimer are very much a part of Kettering in its wider environs and therefore worthy of inclusion. But because the Burton Latimer *Electric Palace* was part of the Watts' Chain of cinemas, then the other cinemas in the chain, The *Regent* at Finedon, and The *Picture Drome* at Irthlingborough are mentioned also, although not in so great a detail. But more importantly, the stories of these little cinemas need to be told to a wider audience than hither-to.

Never a threat to the big houses in Kettering, the little cinemas were loved by those who went there and remembered affectionately by those who ran them. All but one have since passed onto other things, but I found the stories of these little gems fascinating and I am indebted to a number of people who have contributed material. Acknowledgements appear to them at the end of each chapter.

THE ELECTRIC PICTURE PALACE

THE RITZ

DESBOROUGH

Desborough on the A6, six miles north of Kettering was in the latter nineteenth century a small manufacturing town making boots and shoes corsets and mining iron ore. It had its first public hall in 1883 which was near the railway station. It could hold 300 people and had a small stage.

The Oddfellows Hall was built in Station Road by the Desborough Branch of the Manchester Unity of Oddfellows, and it was to become Desborough's main site for entertainment, right up to the present day. It was an imposing building, and from its opening in 1888, the Hall was used for meetings, balls, receptions, public auctions and political hustings.

The Oddfellows' Hall, Desborough, 1890s (T. Smith)

Travelling shows attended the Hall with plays. On Friday 2 December 1897 the Royal Animated Picture Company presented a cinematograph programme which included Queen Victoria's Diamond Jubilee procession (filmed by Acres) and film of a Spanish bullfight. In all over 1,000 feet of film was projected and it would seem that this was the first public paying performance of motion pictures within the Hall and therefore the first 'cinema' performance. Supporting the films as an added attraction were the rendition of appropriate songs by Miss Lillie Mowbray the celebrated contralto.

From 1908 the Hall was let out to theatre companies who frequently presented plays on the well equipped stage. Melodramatic plays including the ever popular *Maria Marten* and *Sweeny Todd, The Demon Barber* were played before enthusiastic Desborough audiences.

By 1910, the Hall became a skating rink, but it was sometime during the night of Friday/Saturday 4/5 November of that year, that a mysterious fire broke out in one of the front offices. Fortunately the flames burned themselves out and the damage was restricted to minor items. The cause of the fire has never been established, though the date may have something to do with it.

In 1912 the Oddfellows Hall was to undergo a major change. Mr and Mrs Jackson of Desborough leased the Hall for use as a cinema. The actual arrangements for the lease are unknown but they are thought to have included some interest by the Oddfellows because they were actively involved as stewards and ushers during the films, and the Oddfellows' Secretary still kept his office on the first floor of the building.

The Hall was provided with sloping floor and seating. The front rows were wooded benches with 'swing backs'. Why swing backs remains a mystery but often the children would reverse the backs and sit looking the other way. The remaining seating was wooden tip-up seats, with plush seats further back. The prices were 2d and 6d.

A large screen was erected on the stage and a grand piano stood to the right. The Secretary's room was divided by a glass partition and the part not occupied by the Secretary became the projection room. A hand cranked projector was installed, thought to be an 'Empire' make. For the electricity, a gas engine was installed under the back of the stage.

The cinema opened as The *Electric Picture Palace*. The event is not recorded in the local press, but at first, performances were nightly at 7.30pm and a matinee on Saturdays. It began a history which was to last for 47 years.

When the Great War began, Harry Jackson was called up, and for a number of years Mrs Jackson ran the cinema. Later she gave up the lease and it would

PROGRAMME. IMPORTANT BOOKINGS!

Mon. June 15. Racing Luck Monty Banks
Thur. „ 18. The Unwanted Lilian Hall-Davies
Mon. „ 22. The Girl, the Devil and the Deep Blue Sea Madge Kennedy
Thur. „ 25. The White Sister Lilian Gish
Mon. „ 29. The Unknown Purple Alice Lake
Thur. July 2. The Girl in the Limousine Larry Seman
Mon. „ 6. The Stranger Betty Compson
Thur. „ 9. The Spitfire Betty Blythe
Mon. „ 13. Big Brother Tom Moore
Thur. „ 16. The Yankee Consul Douglas MacLean
Mon. „ 20. The Heritage of the Desert Bebe Daniels
Thur. „ 23. The Extra Girl Mabel Normand
Mon. „ 27. The Spanish Dancer Pola Negri
Thur. „ 30. The Man with the Iron Mask Vladimir Gaidarow
BANK HOLIDAY.
Mon. Aug. 3. Robin Hood Douglas Fairbanks
Thur. „ 6. Zaza Gloria Swanson
Mon. „ 10. The Night Hawk Harry Carey
Thur. „ 13. Slaves of Destiny Matheson Lang
Mon. „ 17. Richard the Lionhearted Wallace Beery
Thur. „ 20. The Siren [illegible] Seville Priscella Dean
Mon. „ 24. Pied Piper Malone Thomas Meighan
Thur. „ 27. Arabella Mae Marsh
Mon. „ 31. The Midnight Express Elaine Hammerstein
Thur. Sept. 3. The Fire Patrol Madge Bellamy
Mon. „ 7. Her Own Free Will Helene Chadwick
Thur. „ 10. The Speed Spook Johnny Hines
Mon. „ 14. The Great Prince Shan David Hawthorne
Thur. „ 17. Never Say Die Douglas MacLean
DESBOROUGH FEAST.
Mon. „ 21. Ro[illegible] Mary Pickford
Thur. „ 24. Little Robinson Crusoe Jackie Coogan
(Subject to any necessary alteration.)

Also a Fine Selection of 2-Reel Comedies.

ELECTRIC PICTURE PALACE,
Oddfellows' Hall, Desborough.

Marlow & Son, Printers, The Library, Desborough.

Programme of important forthcoming attractions at The Electric Palace. *The date would be about 1922/1923, as the film* Robin Hood *starring Douglas Fairbanks was made in 1922.*

appear that the Oddfellows ran the cinema themselves under the management of the Secretary. By 1926 split week programming was in place with programmes running Monday to Wednesday, and Thursday to Saturday.

There was by then one house Monday to Thursday at 7.30pm and on Friday and Saturday two houses at 6pm and 8.30pm. Children's matinees were shown with shorts and serials. Typical fare is indicated by the programme for Easter 1926 when *Girl Shy* (1924) starring Harold Lloyd was showing Monday to Wednesday and *Boy Of Flanders* (1924) with Jackie Coogan for the rest of the week. The performances usually consisted of a 'B' support picture, a short, a newsreel (usually three weeks old). trailers and then the main feature. Seat prices by now were 3d to 9d.

In 1930 a sound system was installed and with new projectors the first 'talkie' to be shown in the little cinema was *Desert Song* (1929) with John Boles and Carlotta King. This primitive talkie version of the famous operetta had the improved two-colour system. The cinema was packed to capacity every night.

Having a full house however raised a few problems, as there were no toilets in the building. So until ones were provided on the outside in later years, anyone needing to heed nature had to obtain 'pass outs' and use the public toilets opposite.

The interior changed slightly when sound was installed. A new proscenium was erected and was painted with garden scene by a local artist Roy Gotobed. A large roll curtain was fitted on which adverts were placed. This 'roller' was operated by ropes and pulleys by the proscenium, a rather primitive arrangement for the time, but it caused many a smile when as the show was about to start the projectionist Fred Kirby, would pull on the ropes to raise the curtain then go scurrying back to the projection room to start the film. Electrical generating equipment was removed from under the stage and re-sited in a separate building. A glass-roofed canopy was erected over the front of the building to protect queues from the elements.

In September 1937 Mr Roughton Turner sold some land to Robert Neall a cinema proprietor of Daventry, and Claude Copley, a cinema proprietor of Harborough Road, for the purpose of building a new cinema. This was to stir the Oddfellows into offering The *Electric Picture Palace* to the two gentlemen. Copley accepted, and architect Mr Edmund Wilford of Leicester was commissioned to draw up the plans for the complete refurbishment of the old Oddfelows Hall. It was Edmund Wilford who also designed The *Savoy* at Kettering.

Poster for the week beginning Monday 13 September 1937, only weeks before the complete reconstruction as The Ritz

The old entrance was totally reconstructed. A new pay-desk, cloakrooms and plush tip-up seating were installed. The stage was fitted out as for modern cinema and a new proscenium arch was built with modern tabs. The projection room was re-modelled, and the projection equipment and house and stage lighting upgraded.

Externally the frontage had a complete face lift. The old doors and windows were replaced and a modern facade with a central fin replaced the old elevation. The two short semi-circular steps led up to the modern entrance doors above which there was a canopy. The fin carried the new name for the cinema in red and green – The *Ritz*.

The exact date of opening, and the opening programme are not known, but the cinema was a modern, though small counterpart of the larger cinemas in nearby Kettering and Market Harborough. It was to remain in Mr Copley's astute management until 1960, when on Saturday 30 January it closed its doors for the last time as a cinema.

If the old cinema buildings could talk, what tales they might tell. Thankfully there are still people left who can talk for them. In the material sent to me about the Desborough cinema, there is some wonderful narrative which tells us of its life and patrons.

You will remember the description of the seating in the days of The *Electric Picture Palace*, when the first few rows were wooden swing back benches. These rows were called

The Ritz, *about1938* (T. Smith)

the 'chicken-run' and got their name from the antics of children, who, when the lights went out, would crawl underneath rows of benches to find places in the better upholstered seats further back.

In the days of silent films, The *Electric Picture Palace* had quite a grand instrument for which to accompany the films. It was a grand piano, no less, and it was set in an unusual position, on the stage right by the screen. Mostly, accompanists would be below the stage and therefore an easy target for any 'deadeye' patron. The first pianist was George Ginns and occasionally a lady pianist, Clare Brookes.

Behaviour was never always orderly. In the early days the Oddfellows committee provided the ushers. One such was Harry Coe. He was known as 'Hats' Coe because of his pronunciation of the word 'hit', threatening some youngster to sit down or 'I'll hat you if you don't'.

The story goes that one evening during a very sad silent picture, the name is not known, there was a scene which was particularly melodramatic, with the ladies in the audience dabbing moist eyes with hankies and the only sound was the piano reflecting the scene. Suddenly Reggie 'Parbo' Coe, a local youth, released wind rather audibly. The piano stopped playing. The screen went black as the projector stopped running. The lights went on. 'Hats' came marching down to the row where those around Reggie were pointing at him shouting 'It's him, it's him', whereupon the poor unfortunate youth was hoisted from his seat and escorted from the cinema by 'Hats' and told 'you're banned for three months'.

Tom Haycock who is credited with that anecdote also recollected that 'Clubby' Coe (relative to 'Hats' - or Reggie?) used to sit in the front rows puffing on his billowing pipe alongside his posh-talking wife. Tom relates:

> 'Clubby could not read, and relied upon his wife to read off the captions to the silent pictures. On occasions with the noise of the audience he did not hear his wife's commentary and she would have to shout. One such occasion the caption read 'I love you' which Clubby had not heard and she had to repeat it twice in a very loud voice which brought the house down.'

Geoff Marlow remembers The *Electric Picture Palace* of around 1927 and related this amusing account:

> ' As a typical 9 year old of that era, none of my gang had been born in affluence so most of our pastimes were financed by necessity from our own wits. A certain Mr Ginns of Lower King Street used to purchase rabbit skins for a halfpenny a time and kept them in a barn in his garden. We would clamber over his back fence, and 'borrow' a couple of skins, then nip around to his front door for payment upon which he would slip us a penny and invite us to bring him some more. An easy penny to get into the pictures. The same modus operandi was used with spruce (mineral water) bottles at Stenson's shop in Paddock Lane. When these plans failed we had to adopt plan 'B' to get into the pictures by going to the rear wall of the cinema 'gents'. The lavatory had no roof so it was easy to drop inside and then through the door on the left of the cinema. Often we would be spotted by Harry 'Hats' Coe and our rehearsed conversation would be like this; 'Where have you lot come from?' 'The lav Mr Coe', 'I didn't see you come to the front earlier', 'I did, Mr Coe', 'All right sit down and don't kick up a

row'.

The Kirby family was an important part of the old cinema. Fred Kirby senior, described on the posters as the 'Electrical Engineer' looked after the gas engine and dynamo, which, as mentioned, were situated under the stage. Freddie repaired all the gas engines in Desborough, especially those in the factories. Fred Kirby junior was responsible for the projector and showing the films. He was to continue this role into the sound era.

One final contribution comes from Irene M. Faller and is taken from a letter she wrote to the Evening Telegraph in 1984:

> 'My mother's sister, Mrs Fallers and her husband owned The *Electric Palace* before World War 1. Their names were Mr and Mrs Harry Jackson. Whilst my Uncle was away in the armed forces overseas, Auntie sold the cinema as it had become too much for her. My mother sometimes used to play the piano, as there was no sound then. They had quite a character as an usher in the cinema. He used to shout at the local youths when they made a lot of noise calling 'Let's have a bit less order down the front there'.
> It could only have been 'Hats'.

So after 63 years of involvement with the motion picture, The *Electric Picture Palace*, and The *Ritz* ceased to operate as a cinema. Today it is a restaurant,

Finally, why was the facade of The *Ritz* painted brown? Apparently at the start of the 1939 war it was felt that the white fronted building would be easily seen by an enemy plane finding its way via Desborough so it was painted brown. It just never got changed.

Projection and technical equipment:

There are no details of the early projection equipment of 1912. It is known that the projector was hand cranked so it might well have been an 'Empire' Indomitable or something similar. In 1930 a sound system was installed. It was a Morrison sound system and two Kalee 7s were acquired. In 1938 when the cinema was modernized new projectors, thought to be Kalee 8s were installed with Gaumont-Kalee Duosonic heads and amplification equipment.

Acknowledgments to C. T. Marlow; T. Haycock; G. Marlow; S. M. Irons and Mrs W. Ball.

THE PICTURE HOUSE

THE NEW PICTURE HOUSE ROTHWELL

Better known as Rothwell Pictures, the correct name of this little cinema was The *Picture House* and later The *New Picture House*. Rothwell, a small manufacturing town three miles north of Kettering has a long history and is most notable for its 'Rowell Fair' annually celebrating the town charter granted in 1204. Very little, other than that written by Stan White is recorded about the cinema, and I am indebted to him for much of the contents of this chapter.

Rothwell cinema arrived rather later than most in the area. It was converted from the Oddfellows Hall. The Oddfellows Hall had been opened in 1882 at the corner of New Street and Bell Hill. It was used as a general purpose public hall providing facilities for public meetings. It is thought that motion pictures may have been shown there from time to time with travelling Bioscopes, but no firm evidence exists. It is known that Warren East of Kettering toured the area with his 'animated pictures' so possibly he may have visited Rothwell also.

It is not until the 1920s (possibly 1920 itself), that Len Bailey who was a motor engineer, George Kilburn who was an inventor and the 'Water Works' man, together with Arthur Pollard a traveller for a local boot and shoe factory, took over the Oddfellows Hall and converted it into a cinema. It is thought there were several others involved as well.

The front of the cinema was on the corner of the building with the bulk of the brick running back along what I believe was Madams Hill. A photograph of the 1940s shows the entrance façade was of a concrete rendering and judging by the personnel in the picture this must have been after the re-modelling of the cinema. It is believed therefore that the exterior of the cinema had not changed much from earlier days.

Site of the original Oddfellows' Hall and the Picture House *Rothwell, after conversion to a shoe factory*

Entrance to the cinema was by steps up to the pay-desk and then into the auditorium by double doors. The floor was 'raked' in the 1920s conversion, and there was no Balcony. The roof was supported by timber cross arches giving it an almost chapel like appearance, the stage was left more or less where it was and the screen was erected across it.

The modest interior

A projection room was built and reached by an iron ladder which ran up the entrance foyer wall. Two projectors were installed along with a slide lantern. Musical accompaniment was provided by a piano situated somewhere front of the stage, and the pianist's name is not known. Sadly there is no record in the local press or otherwise of the opening day nor of the programmes shown, but open it did and was named The *Picture House*.

Note the roof beams and narrow proscenium

Power for the operation was provided by a gas engine situated in a yard further up New Street, but by 1930, the cinema was on the mains electric supply. At this time it was thought that sound was installed. The projectionists at the time were William York and Alby Green.

At this point, any historical detail is unavailable, so we can only therefore move on to take up the story immediately after the Second World War.

Sometime during 1945, The *Picture House* was taken over by Hudson Cinemas and was closed for refurbishment. The exterior of the entrance received its concrete rendering and was fitted out with new stills displays and other cinema paraphernalia. The interior was refurbished, and the seating re-arranged in such a way as to remove the slight obstructions caused previously by roof support pillars. The cinema re-opened with a new name The *New Picture House*. It is not clear whether there was a refurbishment of the proscenium arch at this time.

The Hudson circuit ran the cinema, by employing a father and son team whose name is unknown, but after two years they moved on to be replaced by John Harvey who hailed from Sheringham. The projection team at this time was Lionel Collins, Dennis Scotney and Stan White. The cinema opened once nightly at 7.30pm. On Saturday there were two shows, with the first house starting at 5.30pm and then a second about 8.30pm. In 1948 the Hudsons sold the cinema and the new owners were registered as the Rothwell Cinema Company. It was at this time that the little cinema was to have its golden years.

The projectionist, Lewis Collins in 1947

The new manager was Eric Gillette who took control of the cinema a few weeks after its sale. He was a good manager and made several improvements. The old iron ladder was replaced with proper stairs and door which led onto the steps leading from the main entrance up to the pay desk. A new screen was installed, as were two new projectors. It is not certain whether Gillette refurbished the interior, but photographs show the auditorium as having a wooden panelling part way up the wall and an open panelling for the remainder. Wall lights seem to be the main lighting and included secondary lighting. The proscenium was of fluted design and the screen tabs were of a heavy maroon material. The ceiling and roof supports remained as before.

Eric Gillette changing the 'stills' display. Late 1940s

By the 1950s The *New Picture House* was nearing its end, and at the beginning of 1951 the writing was on the wall. The projectionist of the time, Colin Bamford, describes the final days:

> 'I had gone in on a Wednesday afternoon to do the programme for the following day to find Eric [Gillette] on the telephone to the film renters in Birmingham, and obviously having problems. I also noticed letters from Kalee and Automaticket complaining of slow payments. Then the inevitable happened a few weeks later when I again went in to make up the programme, Eric told me to take a poster 'closed until further notice' and paste it on the billboard over the door, and that was that.'

Projectionists Stan White and Bill York. Late 1940s

The cinema closed on Saturday 19 February 1951. The last film shown on its screen was *Mask Of The Gorilla* (1944). A fitting end.

Colin Bamforth describes the bitter end for the 'little gem' that was Rothwell pictures. A little time after the closure he went to the sale of effects. He recalls;

> 'I'll always remember that day. Sonny Pentelow brought the electric clock. It hadn't worked for weeks. Someone brought the amplifier for 10s, complete with the cinema speakers, and they smashed them up just to get at the metal parts. Only the best seats, those at the back, were bought, including the doubles. The projectors were sold to The *Orion* Cinema at Market Harborough ands I think the screen also. I've often wondered why the cinema needed to go bust.'

The site eventually became Taylor's factory and presently is a business making electrical components. As for Eric Gillette, he went north to manage some major cinemas before going into business on his own. He retired to South Wales. Colin Bamforth lives in Australia, and Stan White still lives in Rothwell.

Projection and technical information:

The first projectors in 1920 were two American built Simplex mute projectors with front shutters. The light source was carbon arc and they were not integrally a part of the projector. The projectors were from an American patent dated 1916 and would have been manufactured around that time.

There is no date as to when the sound was installed but it was apparently a simple system using Morrison sound heads to the Simplex projectors. Apparently this system was troublesome with dirt and emulsion flakes from the film collecting in the exciter system causing loss of sound and therefore required regular cleaning during projection. The Simplex projectors remained until 1948 when they were replaced by two Kalee 8 projectors. They must have been the oldest running front-shutter machines in the county.

It is not known whether the sound system was changed but it is supposed that probably Westrex heads came with the replacement projectors. A slide lantern was part of the projection equipment and was used right up to the closing for showing local business advertisements. There would appear to have been only two screens installed, the first in 1920, and the second in 1948.

Acknowledgements to Stan White, Lewis John Stanley and Colin Bamforth.

The original Simplex projector

Kalee 8 projector which replaced the Simplex

A TYPICAL MONTHLY PROGRAMME AT THE NEW PICTURE HOUSE

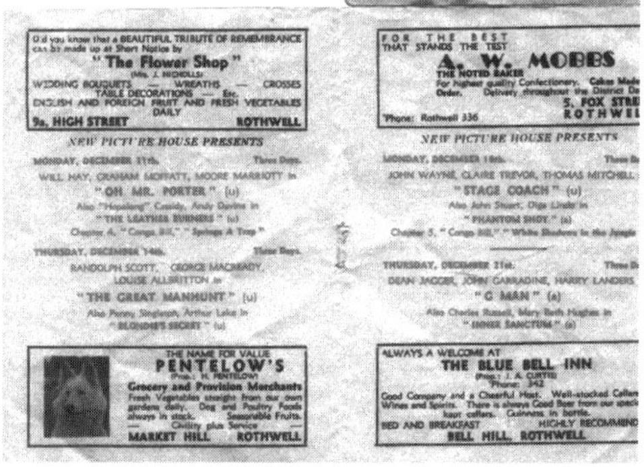

"The Flower Shop"
WEDDING BOUQUETS — WREATHS — CROSSES
TABLE DECORATIONS — Etc.
ENGLISH AND FOREIGN FRUIT AND FRESH VEGETABLES DAILY
9a, HIGH STREET ROTHWELL

NEW PICTURE HOUSE PRESENTS

"OH MR. PORTER" (u)

"THE GREAT MANHUNT" (u)

THE NAME FOR VALUE
PENTELOW'S
Grocery and Provision Merchants
MARKET HILL ROTHWELL

FOR THE BEST THAT STANDS THE TEST
A. W. MOBBS
THE NOTED BAKER
'Phone: Rothwell 336

NEW PICTURE HOUSE PRESENTS

"STAGE COACH" (u)

"G MAN" (a)

ALWAYS A WELCOME AT
THE BLUE BELL INN
BED AND BREAKFAST
BELL HILL, ROTHWELL

A typical monthly programme at The Picture House. *Early 1950s*

THE ELECTRIC PALACE

THE BENTLEY

THE OHIO

BURTON LATIMER

'What's on at Watts'. That catchy little slogan was the keyword to cinemagoers in the A6 towns of Burton Latimer, Finedon and Irthlingborough. It was coined by Alfred Watts when he took over The *Electric Palace* in Burton Latimer in 1924.

In Burton Latimer, local shoe manufacturers Joseph Westley and Henry Whitney joined with the plumbing engineer A. G. Miller and formed a company, the Burton Latimer Electric Palace Company. In 1914 the company built a cinema off the High Street, behind what was then a coffee house and public hall, and called it The *Electric Palace*, which duly opened on an unknown date in August.

Entrance to the cinema was from the High Street through an arch of semi-circular Romanesque design and constructed of segmented masonry. THE

PALACE was etched in the masonry above the arch work and the buttresses were of stone block each with a large electric globe for illumination. On each buttress was an illustrated stills cabinet and the archway could be closed off by two wooden gates. The cinema was behind the High Street and reached by a rise to the entrance on the right. This was particularly useful as it was a holding area for queues although not under cover.

The cinema and its interior was designed by the architect R. J. Williams of Kettering to a high standard of spaciousness and comfort. Entering the foyer the pay-desk was immediately to hand and to the left and right doors into the auditorium. The cinema seated 500 and was approximately 52 feet long by 37 feet wide. The rake of the floor was about three feet from screen to rear, and the seats ranged from wooden benches at the front to red plush tip-up at the rear.

The cinema was built with its own generating plant which also powered the electric globes let into the plaster work ceiling. It was heated by the new style 'high flow' system, which is taken to mean an improved water radiator of the time.

The archway through to The Electric Palace. *The main building can be seen ahead with the entrance to the cinema on the right*

The *Electric Palace* had opened quietly in August 1914. No press advertisements can be found until November. It is possible that the outbreak of the Great War had something to do with it, but on the week starting Monday 2 November 1914 a fully advertised programme was shown, and which is generally regarded as the 'official opening'.

The week was a split week and on Monday, Tuesday and Wednesday the programme was *Zigomar* (1914) a crime melodrama with Paul Brochet; the comedy *Mrs Finch And Nephew Billy* (1913); the dramas *Pure Puritive Model* (1912) and *Senators Bill* (1914); and two Keystone comedies *A Barnyard Flirtation* (1913) and *Politeness Pays* (1913). Latest newsreels from the war front were also shown.

Thursday to Saturday the programme was *The Honour Of The Law* (1914); *Seagull* (1913); *Murray's Wedding Present* and *Sandy And Shorty* (dates not known); *Start Something* (1913) and *Pimple Pinched* (1912) together with the latest war pictures.

Of the first night the report was laudable saying:

> 'The opening of the new picture house in Burton Latimer, The Electric Palace, last August has seen its popularity increase by leaps and bounds. It is attractive with its curved arch and electric lamps casting a flood of light over the High Street. Once inside one is aware of its spaciousness and comfort. The programme on Monday officially opened the cinema.'

The projectionist was Mr 'Mac' Goodman, and later Mr 'Tut' Clipston. Mr Wilfred Miller, brother of one of the partners, A. G. Miller, was the pianist, and over the years other pianists were Wilfred Sturman, Cecil Hickman and Ada Wood. The film programmes were changed twice weekly, a format which remained until 1924, with performances at 8pm from Monday to Friday, and 2.30pm, 7pm and 9pm on Saturdays.

In 1922, the running of the cinema was taken over by Mr David Strutley He continued, until the cinema was sold to Alfred Watts in 1924, who eventually was to own a small chain of three cinemas.

Alfred Watts ran the cinema until 1938 when his son Geoff took over the chain as Watts Cinemas Limited. He continued the slogan 'What's on at Watts' which featured in all published programmes.

In 1955 The *Electric Palace* at Burton Latimer was re-equipped with a wide screen, along with a refurbishment, but in 1960, because of falling attendances, it was closed, along with the two others in the Watts' chain. There were moves to encourage the Burton Latimer Urban Distinct Council to acquire the property, but this came to nothing.

WET FISH and POTATOES
Mon., Tues., Wed., Thurs. 8 a.m. — 1 p.m.
Friday and Saturday 8 a.m. — 1-30 p.m.

FOR THE BEST VALUE IN FISH & CHIPS
THE FISH SALOON
Fried under the Most Hygienic Conditions.
(Mr. E. J. Smith)
13 STATION ROAD, BURTON LATIMER

FISH AND CHIPS
Mon., Tues., Wed., Thurs. 4-30 to 10-30 p.m.
Friday 11-30 — 1-30 p.m. and 4-30 — 10-30 p.m.
Saturday 11-30 — 1-30 p.m. and 6-0 — 10-30 p.m.

Monday, June 1st — Two Days
Don Kelly, Barbara Luna in
VALLEY OF DEATH Ⓤ
Joan Rice in The Long Knife Ⓤ

Wednesday, June 3rd — Two Days
Frank Sinatra, Tony Curtis in
KINGS GO FORTH Ⓐ
Also Full Supporting Programme

Friday, June 5th — Three Days
Virginia McKenna, Bill Travers in Ⓐ
PASSIONATE SUMMER E'col.
Peter Reynolds, The Bank Raiders Ⓤ

Monday, June 8th — Two Days
Barbara Shelley in CAT GIRL Ⓧ
Wally Campo, Hell Squad Ⓧ

Wednesday, June 10th — Two Days
Audie Murphy in E'color
RIDE A CROOKED TRAIL Ⓤ
George Nader, The Big Story Ⓐ

Friday, June 12h — Two Days
Victor Mature in CHINA DOLL Ⓐ
Also Louis Armstrong in
Satchmo The Great Ⓤ

Monday, June 15th — Two Days
Rory Calhoun in E'color
SAGA OF HEMP BROWN
Also John Agar in
The Mole People Ⓐ

Wednesday, June 17th — Two Days
Tony Curtis, Sidney Poitier in
THE DEFIANT ONES Ⓐ
Also Full Supporting Programme

Friday, June 19th — Two Days
Michael Redgrave, Tony Britton in Ⓐ
BEHIND THE MASK E'color
Rex Allen in Utah Wagon Train Ⓤ

Monday, June 22nd — Two Days
John Saxon, Sandra Dee in
THE WONDERFUL YEARS Ⓐ
Ray Danton in The Night Runner Ⓐ

Wednesday, June 24th — Two Days
Virginia Maskell, John Cassavetes in
E'color VIRGIN ISLAND Ⓤ
Also Full Supporting Programme

Friday, June 26th — Two Days
Richard Attenborough John Gregson
SEA OF SAND
Wm. Sylvester in Dublin Nightmare Ⓤ

Monday, June 29th — Two Days
Audie Murphy in
THE GUN RUNNERS Ⓐ
Also Woman of Mystery Ⓤ

IT'S THE GARAGE WITH A SERVICE THAT COUNTS — BE WISE, CALL OR PHONE
HAYNE'S GARAGE
FOR COMPLETE SATISFACTION
KETTERING ROAD, BURTON LATIMER

High Pressure Greasing
Castrol Oils
Complete Overhauls
Welding, Spares, etc.
Tel. Burton Latimer 256
We Stock & Recommend
CLEVELAND PETROL

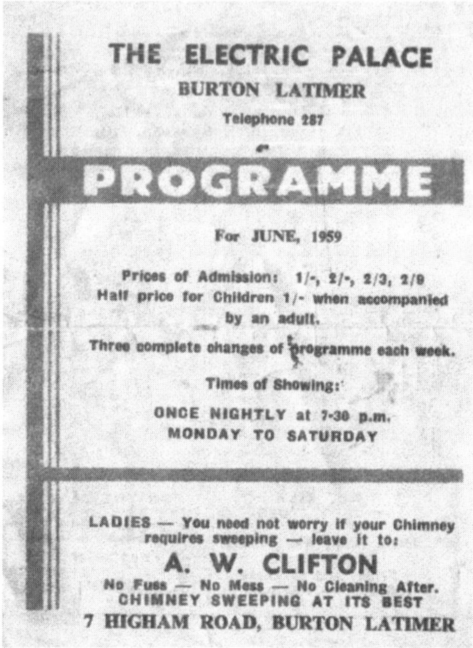

THE ELECTRIC PALACE
BURTON LATIMER
Telephone 287

PROGRAMME

For JUNE, 1959

Prices of Admission: 1/-, 2/-, 2/3, 2/9
Half price for Children 1/- when accompanied by an adult.
Three complete changes of programme each week.
Times of Showing:
ONCE NIGHTLY at 7-30 p.m.
MONDAY TO SATURDAY

LADIES — You need not worry if your Chimney requires sweeping — leave it to:
A. W. CLIFTON
No Fuss — No Mess — No Cleaning After.
CHIMNEY SWEEPING AT ITS BEST
7 HIGHAM ROAD, BURTON LATIMER

A monthly programme for June 1959

Some time after the closure, the building was taken over by Mr Thomas Dodds of Findeon, and opened as a Bingo hall, the Rutland Bingo Hall. This also subsequently closed and the building was unused for several years.

In 1985 Ashley Whyatt brought the building for £50,000, carried out a major restoration, and in January 1986, opened as a cinema using the name of The *Bentley*, an amalgamation of his own name with that of his wife Bente. The cinema however closed in 1987, and the building was sealed up, and fell into dereliction.

Mr Brian McFarlane, who was now owner of The *Ohio* twin cinemas in Kettering, took over the derelict cinema in 1994, and changed the interior and entrance way, bringing this, together with a small foyer, around to the other side of the building effectively doing away with the original entrance via High Street. The entrance now was from the car park off Churchill Way. The interior

The Ohio *in 1997, with the newly constructed main entrance on the side*

The old archway, still in existence

was halved with the seating reduced to 50 or so. The seating décor and equipment were renewed and this cosy little cinema was re-opened under the name of The *Ohio*.

Sadly this was not to be successful either, and the cinema closed soon afterwards. However, we perhaps have a happy ending, for the building, at least. In 1998, there was a complete remodelling and refurbishment, making it almost unrecognisable from the original. It is now an Italian restaurant, Guiseppe's, and very good it is too, the author testifying by personal experience.

The building today after a complete remodelling. It is now an Italian restaurant

The Watts chain of the three cinemas was in existence from 1924 to 1960, and provided cinema entertainment for the three A6 shoe towns of Burton Latimer, Finedon and Irthlingborough. The programmes for the three cinemas changed three times a week, achieved by the rotation of three films per week through the three cinemas in the chain. All the cinemas showed only one performance per night, but two on a Saturday, and one house on Sunday.

The Watts' chain two other cinemas were The *Regent* at Finedon, and The *Picture Drome* at Irthlingborough. The *Regent* cinema at Finedon was originally the Methodist chapel in Regent Street, hence the name. It was built in 1822, but by 1904 had ceased to be a chapel, and was converted into the boot and shoe factory of Dunkley and Shrive. In 1928, Alfred Watts acquired the building and converted it into The *Regent* cinema.

When the Watts chain finished operations in 1960, the cinema was used as a paper warehouse by a Leicester paper firm. It is since been converted into a private dwelling.

The *Picture Drome* at Irthlingborough, became a cinema about the same time, the late 1920s, as the ones at Finedon and Burton Latimer. It is known to have had a modernisation and refurbishment sometime in the 1950s. The building is now boarded up, although there are plans that it may be opened as an Irthlingborough Community Centre.

The Regent *today, as a private dwelling*

The boarded up Picture Drome. *There may be plans to turn it into a Community Centre*

PART SIX

THE CINEMA CLOCKS

Towards the end of my research, someone mentioned to me about the clocks which were installed in most of the Kettering cinemas, and I remembered that those timepieces were quite distinctive. Not only were they an important part of the service for patrons, but also advertisements for themselves, or businesses in the town. I was unable to find any records of the clocks, so I have to rely solely on memory, which I hope serves me correctly.

It is important to realise the significance of having clocks in cinemas of those days. Ownership of wrist watches was not common. It is true that many men in those days had a pocket watch, on an 'Albert', which was often handed down from father to son, but for a young lad to receive such a watch either as a present or heirloom was rare. Children almost never had a watch. In those days the performances were continuous, and getting there often required public transport. It was therefore of great importance for cinemas to display the time, as it was possible to lose track of the hour in the long performances, and thus miss the last bus home.

Today, with everyone having their own timepieces and cars, the modern multiplex auditoria do not need to provide this service though some older cinemas in the country may still do so.

THE ODEON

Virtually in any one of Oscar Deutch's *Odeons* you would find the same design of clock. They were a part of the corporate image. The Kettering Odeon was no exception, with one face each side of the proscenium arch. The familiar octagonal face used the words ODEON THEATRE for the twelve hours. ODEON was spelt out clockwise, starting with the O at the 10 position, D at 11, E at 12 and so on until the N was at 2. The word THEATRE started at the 9 position and went anti-clockwise with H at 8 E at 7 until the final E was at 3.

The face was illuminated in red and the hands and letters were black. There may have been another similar clock in the cinema but I cannot remember one., as the proscenium clock was clearly visible from both Stalls and Circle.

THE REGAL

The Regal clocks were rather elegant affairs. The face was etched on to a pale green glass and illuminated by a strip lighting incorporated into the top of the clock frame. The figures were in Arabic numerals and a script style fount. The outline of the face was shaped in the form of an octagon. The words REGAL KETTERING were etched on to the face outside of the clock area. Figures and words were in black.

There were two clocks in the vast auditorium. One was in the centre of the wall at the rear of the Stalls, and the second was in the centre of the rear Circle wall. If you wanted to check the time whilst seated, you had to turn your head and upper body fully around which was something just a little annoying to the person immediately behind. I seem also to remember there was another clock in the foyer and one in the restaurant.

There were a number of 'Regal' clocks in shops around the town and certainly in a butchers' shop in the High Street. I think it was Carlton's although I am not too sure.

THE GRANADA

When Granada Theatres took over, they retained the clocks and just removed The *Regal* name. The 'Regal' clocks around the town just disappeared (has anybody got one?). It is strange that the clocks were not replaced, but I recollect that the number of *Granadas* I worked in, did not have any sort of corporate image timepiece which was odd for such a prestigious company.

THE EMPIRE

There was only one clock in this little cinema and that was situated on the left side of the proscenium. Typical of many clocks in smaller cinemas, The *Empire* instrument was housed in an elongated case, black in colour, the upper part containing the clock face and the lower portion displaying an advertisement for a local business, the name of which I cannot remember.

The clock face spelled out EMPIRE CINEMA instead of the numerals and they were in black as were the hands. The whole was illuminated in either orange or red. I think the clock may have changed in the later years.

THE SAVOY

Two clocks were situated either side of the wide proscenium. They were very similar to The *Regal* clocks in appearance but I think the faces were etched with numerals within a square. I again do not remember specifically, but I am sure that the word SAVOY was also etched on to the glass work. The figures and hands were black against the pale green background.

On the left side of the proscenium when facing it, near to the clock was a programme indicator, which would light up the number of the act performing on the stage corresponding to the printed programme. The indicator was very up-to-date for the times, and even today would appear very acceptable as a piece of electronic equipment. The numbers were displayed on a matrix in pleasing digital style.

THE GAUMONT PAVILION

I dimly remember a clock on the left hand side of the proscenium, but as to its design, I am unsure. I think it had some reference to GB probably in the GB logo style. I cannot recollect there being a clock in the refurbished Gaumont.

THE WORKING MEN'S CLUB

Worthy of mention is the old clock that hung over the entrance doors inside the Concert Room of the Club where the cinema performances were held. It was a round wooden clock, at the bottom of which was a curved door which opened to reveal the small pendulum. The face was white and circular and the numerals in black Roman style. Overhead was a small light. Inscribed across the dial was the maker's name, I cannot remember what it was but I am sure it was of a local clockmaker. With a glass front it was the typical clock of clubs and pubs of the time.

THE FINAL REEL

This book is a celebration of the Kettering cinemas and not a lament on their passing, though sadly not one of the originals remains. It is easy to say that television has killed them off or that sex films were to blame. To some extent that is true, but it goes deeper than that.

In the 1950s television made inroads into the picture-going habit especially when colour television arrived. The film industry retaliated by presenting films in different formats on bigger and better screens, experiences which were just not possible on miniscule television screens.

This new technology, however could not halt the demise of the cinemas, and Kettering cinema seating capacity dropped from over 5,000 seats to less than 500 in 1997. And then, for the best part of one year, Kettering had no cinema at all, and that at a that time when cinema was thriving elsewhere.

There are two major reasons why Kettering lost its centrally located cinemas. Business factors and lack of support. The reason for both The *Gaumont* and The *Odeon* closing was quite simply that there was more profit to be made in property deals than in showing pictures. This was obviously a formidable core argument in closing both cinemas, which were owned by the same organisation, even though they were doing acceptable business at the time of closure, The *Gaumont* especially. In its place we now have a rank of ugly shops, and where the *Odeon* stood, a shopping centre of little character.

The loss of The *Granada* is probably the saddest of all. Perhaps it was too large for a single screen cinema. but it was no dinosaur. With a little enterprise it could have been transformed into a film centre, and would have sustained some entertainment facility in a town centre which is now bereft of anything resembling social life.

'Costs too high' I hear you cry. But did the conversion to Bingo and subsequent renovations cost nothing? Closure was simply business - to capitalise without enterprise. Statements made at the time of the closure to obtain a Bingo licence reveal the argument as being 'to get a Bingo licence…to protect the Company's commercial interest. It is far too early to go into detail [about the future plans]'. That, of course, said it all and the Town Council of the day fell for it.

Business interests were not the only reason. The townspeople were also responsible, by their lack of support, which is the other major factor for the loss of cinemas. The poor old *Empire* cried out to survive but was killed off by public apathy. Even as a second-run art cinema it had opportunities if it had been supported. Small, cosy and intimate, it could have been with us today as a community run venue, similar to the one I support today. Unfortunately it was abandoned, first to a warehouse and then to the needs of the omnivorous motor car. Even the name has been obliterated from its remains.

The *Ohio* cinemas in the old *Savoy* building closed for the same reason. As I left the twin cinemas after meeting Brian McFarlane in 1966, I was witness to the death throes, at a time when cinema was booming elsewhere. Two excellent films were programmed, but only two people turned up to see the film in *Screen* 1, and Brian had to close *Screen 2* because of total lack of patronage. Why was this so?

Later that evening, talking to some young people, I was told that 'no one goes to The *Ohio*. It's too old. We all go to Milton Keynes' It was tragic, and I left them, angry. The piquant words of one of The *Granada* staff on the day that it closed, serves as an epitaph to all the cinemas: 'Kettering people do not know what they want. No matter what shows you put on they are not even interested enough to find out what we are showing, or care' Bitter words, very sad, and very likely, true.

As I close this book I learn of the likely demolition of the old *Savoy* building. How sad that this could not have been saved for community use. Still a fine built theatre, it would be a great loss to the town, and all of the Kettering theatre and cinema heritage will be gone forever. It's The *Odeon* and Central Hall all over again. When will the custodians of Kettering wake up and learn?

All is not gloomy however, for although it is out of the town centre, the new *Odeon* 8-Screen Multiplex is a fine successor to the old Kettering cinemas. It is situated on the edge of town and very convenient for the mobile who are well catered for by it. But what about those without mobility, the elderly and the children? Is there adequate public transport? This is essential if those members of the community are not to be denied a visit to the cinema.

So the story of cinema-going in Kettering has not quite ended yet. With the new *Odeon*, the provision of motion-picture entertainment at Kettering seems to be in safe hands for the foreseeable future, although it is ironic to realise that, with eight screens, Kettering now has more 'cinemas' than it has ever had at any one time. The *Odeon* deserves long life and success.

To the people of Kettering who have a love of the motion-picture, and those who want to see movies as they can only be really appreciated - on a cinema screen - I say, use it, don't lose it.

GLOSSARY

Some of the terms used in the text may be unfamiliar. A short glossary is therefore given

Anamorphic Lens
A lens fitted to a camera for filming and to a projector for screening which effectively 'squeezes' the image for the Cinemascope process. The picture width on projection was between 2.35 (for normal optical sound track) and 2.55 (for magnetic stereophonic sound) times the picture height.

Cinemascope
The trade name for the above 'squeezing' process. Although known in the early silent days, the process was developed by Twentieth Century Fox in the early 1950s, who registered the name, and brought it into regular use.

Cine-Variety
Programmes which included stage acts between film shows.

Day Sets
The 'trailers' such as 'Coming All Next Week' or 'Future Presentations At This Cinema' and so on, usually incorporating the cinema logo.

Film Sets
The opposite of Cine-Variety, film sets were the films between the stage shows.

Fly
The area above a theatre stage from where the scenery and tabs were dropped onto the stage. Purpose built cinemas therefore did not need flies, and would use curtains to dress the stage for any live performance.

Flood
A Floodlight.

Gaff
Usually tented and portable theatres, As permanent theatres and halls were built, the gaffs became extinct.

House
The term used to describe the status of a cinema, AA being the most prestigious, down to B. In Kettering there were no AAs. The *Regal, Gaumont* and *Odeon* were As, whilst The *Empire* and *Savoy* were Bs.
Also describes the number of that day's performance, ie the First House at 6pm, the Second House at 8.30pm.
Letterbox
The notice boards outside the cinema advertising the films. So called because the titles were made up with metal or wooden letters slid into a framework called the letter box. Today some cinemas still use this system either mechanical or electrical.
Myrioama
A staged entertainment consisting of a number of views or tableaux with music and speech. The cinematograph was used extensively in these shows which were very popular in Victorian and Edwardian times.
Non-Sync.
The sound system that is not synchronized to the film sound reproduction though it may use the same amplification system. A term used to describe the equipment used for playing discs or 'tapes' for interval music.
Proscenium
The stage opening. The decoration around and above the stage is the proscenium arch.
Rear Projection
When the projector is behind the screen, thus requiring a system of prisms or mirrors to get the image the 'right way round'. The screen has to be of a special translucent fabric. There are few (if any) rear projection cinemas today, although the system is still quite common in film, television and studio production, and for large stage productions.
Projectormatic
An automated projection instrument with a 'pegged' drum on to which the operation of a whole film programme, or a whole day of film programmes, could be pre-arranged, and thus, without the need for human intervention, start and stop projectors, open curtains and so on. With modern computer systems, it is now obsolete.
Panavision
Another trade name for the Cinemascope process.
Reel
The term by which cinema is measured.. In the old days, one reel contained about 1,000 feet of rolled up film. The running time for a reel of film

obviously depended on the speed at which it was photographed, but since the advent of sound and running at 24 frames per second, the average projection time for one reel of 1,000 feet was 11 minutes, Any film that lasted more than 11 minutes therefore would need more than one reel, so would be termed two-reelers, three-reelers and so on.

Scena

A scenario

Split Week

The division of the week into separate programmes, usually Monday to Wednesday and Thursday to Saturday. Some cinemas would split into three (the Watts' chain did) of Monday and Tuesday; Wednesday and Thursday; Friday and Saturday.

Sound chamber

Usually behind the screen where the loudspeakers were.

Stereophonic Sound

Where the sound is reproduced from the general area of the screen where the action and dialogue is taking place. Thus the speech of characters wherever placed on the screen, appeared to come from them, and no one else. Though systems were in use for many years, stereophonic sound became more widespread with the advent of 3-D films and with Cinemascope, especially in the 2:55 to 1 ratio where four sound tracks on the film were reproduced from the left, centre and right speakers behind the screen, and the 'effects' speakers from around the auditorium

Spot

A spotlight, and a 'moving spot' which could follow actors around the stage.

Tabs

The curtains, usually 'front tabs' for the proscenium and 'screen tabs' for the actual screen

Three Dimension (3-D)

Anaglyphic:

A system giving 'depth' to films using two colour image separation, usually red and green (or blue/green) , where the red is only seen by the left eye. Used in the late 1930s for novelty films. Still available today with 8mm films

Natural Vision:

A system developed by using left and right filtering at the filming stage and again at the screening stage. The projectors showed a separate left copy and right copy of the film each tightly synchronized. Viewing was by a pair of Polaroid spectacles slightly tinted, similar to sun glasses. The system often had a separate film carrying a magnetic sound track. Warner Brothers popularized 3-D with their film *House of Wax* and all together something over 50 films were made in this format. Today there is a single film copying image either with 'layover' or side by side, plus of course, the up and coming computer graphics.

VistaVision:

A non-amorphic process which shot film on 70mm (usual gauge of cinema film is 35mm) two frames together horizontally. In some cinemas the film was shown on special 70mm equipment but for general release the film was reduced to the normal 35mm vertical frame enabling it to be shown on normal projectors. The result was a high definition picture in which the background was as clear as the fore ground. It was advertised as 'motion picture high fidelity'. Cinemascope responded by filming on 55mm film and reducing to 35mm, and calling it Cinemascope 55.